200 Light
vegetarian dishes

hamlyn | **all color cookbook**

200 **Light**
vegetarian dishes

An Hachette UK Company
www.hachette.co.uk

First published in Great Britain in 2015 by Hamlyn
a division of Octopus Publishing Group Ltd
Endeavour House, 189 Shaftesbury Avenue
London WC2H 8JY
www.octopusbooks.co.uk
www.octopusbooksusa.com

Copyright © Octopus Publishing Group Ltd 2015

Distributed in the US by Hachette Book Group,
1290 Avenue of the Americas, 4th and 5th Floors,
New York, NY 10020

Distributed in Canada by Canadian Manda Group,
664 Annette St., Toronto, Ontario, Canada M6S 2C8

Recipes in this book have previously appeared in other books by Hamlyn.

All rights reserved. No part of this book may be reproduced or utilized in any form or by any means, electronic or mechanical, including photocopying, recording, or by any information storage or retrieval system, without the prior written permission of the publisher.

ISBN: 978-0-600-62973-3

Printed and bound in China.

1 2 3 4 5 6 7 8 9 10

Standard level spoon measurements are used in all recipes.

Ovens should be preheated to the specified temperature. If using a convection oven, follow the manufacturer's instructions for adjusting the time and temperature.

Fresh herbs, medium eggs, and freshly ground black pepper should be used unless otherwise stated.

This book includes dishes made with nuts and nut derivatives. It is advisable for people with known allergic reactions to nuts and nut derivatives, or those who may be potentially vulnerable to these allergies, such as pregnant and nursing mothers, invalids, the elderly, babies, and children, to avoid dishes made with these. It is prudent to check the labels of all ready-made ingredients for the possible inclusion of nut derivatives.

contents

introduction	6
recipes under 200 calories	18
recipes under 300 calories	70
recipes under 400 calories	142
recipes under 500 calories	200
index	236
acknowledgments	240

introduction

introduction

this series

The Hamlyn All Color Light Series is a collection of handy-sized books, each packed with more than 200 healthy recipes in a variety of cuisines and topics to suit your needs.

The books are designed to help those people who are trying to lose weight by offering a range of delicious recipes that are low in calories but still high in flavor. The recipes show a calorie count per portion, so you will know exactly what you are eating. These are recipes for real and delicious food, not ultra-deprivation meals, so they will help you maintain your new healthier eating plan for life. They must be used as part of a balanced diet, with the cakes and sweet dishes eaten only as an occasional treat.

how to use this book

All the recipes in this book are clearly marked with the number of calories (kcal) per serving. The chapters cover different calorie bands: under 500 calories, under 400 calories, and so on. There are variations on each recipe at the bottom of the page. Pay attention to the calorie count because they do vary and can sometimes be more than the original recipe.

The figures assume that you are using low-fat versions of dairy products, so be sure to use skim milk and low-fat yogurt. They have also been calculated using lean meat, so make sure you trim meat of all visible fat and remove the skin from chicken breasts. Use moderate amounts of oil and butter for cooking and low-fat/low-calorie alternatives whenever you can.

Don't forget to take note of the number of portions each recipe makes and divide up the quantity of food accordingly, so that you know exactly how many calories you are consuming.

Be careful about accompaniments and any sides that will also add to the calorie content.

Above all, enjoy trying out the new flavors and exciting recipes that this book has to offer. And instead of dwelling on the thought that you are denying yourself your usual unhealthy treats, think of your new regime as a positive step toward a new you. Not only will you lose weight and feel more confident as a result, but your health will benefit, the

condition of your hair and nails will improve, and you will take on a healthy glow.

the risks of obesity

Up to half of women and two-thirds of men are overweight or obese in the developed world today. Being overweight can not only make us unhappy with our appearance, but can also lead to serious health problems, including heart disease, high blood pressure, and diabetes.

When someone is obese, it means they are overweight to the point that it could start to seriously threaten their health. In fact, obesity ranks as a close second to smoking as a possible cause of cancer. Obese women are more likely to have complications during and after pregnancy, and people who are overweight or obese are also more likely to suffer from coronary heart disease, gallstones, osteoarthritis, high blood pressure, and type 2 diabetes.

how can I tell if I am overweight?

The best way to tell if you are overweight is to work out your body mass index (BMI). There are a number of BMI calculators online you can use, or you can do it yourself using the following formula. Divide your weight in pounds (lb) by your height in inches (in) times itself, then multiply by 703. So, if you weigh 180 lb and are 68 inches tall, the calculation would be 180 ÷ 4,624 x 703 = 27.3. Compare the result with the list below (these figures apply to healthy adults only).

Less than 20	underweight
20–25	healthy
26–30	overweight
Over 31	obese

As we all know by now, one of the major causes of obesity is eating too many calories.

what is a calorie?

One of the major causes of obesity is eating too many calories. Of course our bodies need energy in order to stay alive, grow, keep warm, and undertake activities. We get the energy we need to survive from the food and drinks we consume—more specifically, from the fat, carbohydrate, protein, and alcohol they contain.

A calorie (cal), as any dieter can tell you, is the unit used to measure how much energy

different foods contain. A calorie can be scientifically defined as the energy required to raise the temperature of 1 gram of water by 1°C (or 1.8°F) at normal atmospheric pressure. A kilocalorie (kcal) is 1,000 calories and it is, in fact, kilocalories that we usually mean when we talk about the calories in food.

Different food types contain different numbers of calories. For example, a gram of carbohydrate (starch or sugar) provides 3.75 kcal, protein provides 4 kcal per gram, fat provides 9 kcal per gram, and alcohol provides 7 kcal per gram. So, fat is the most concentrated source of energy—weight for weight, it provides just over twice as many calories as either protein or carbohydrate—with alcohol not far behind. The energy content of a food or drink depends on how many grams of carbohydrate, fat, protein, and alcohol are present.

how many calories do we need?

The number of calories we need to consume varies from person to person, but your body weight is a clear indication of whether you are eating the right amount. Body weight is simply determined by the number of calories you are eating compared to the number of calories your body is using to maintain itself and to perform physical activities. If you regularly consume more calories than you use up, you will start to gain weight because extra energy is stored in the body as fat.

Based on our relatively inactive modern-day lifestyles, most nutritionists recommend that women should aim to consume around 2,000 calories (kcal) per day and men an amount of around 2,500. Of course, the amount of energy required depends on your level of activity: the more active you are, the more energy you need to maintain a stable weight.

a healthier lifestyle

To maintain a healthy body weight, we need to expend as much energy as we consume. To lose weight, energy expenditure must therefore exceed intake of calories, so exercise is a vital tool in the fight to lose weight. Physical activity doesn't just help control body weight; it also helps reduce appetite and is known to have beneficial effects on the heart and blood, which will help protect against cardiovascular disease.

Many adults claim not to enjoy doing exercise or say that they simply don't have

Some activities will use up more energy than others. The following list shows some examples of the energy a person weighing 132 lb would expend doing the following activities for 30 minutes:

Activity	Energy
Ironing	69 kcal
Cleaning	75 kcal
Walking	99 kcal
Golf	129 kcal
Fast walking	150 kcal
Cycling	180 kcal
Aerobics	195 kcal
Swimming	195 kcal
Running	300 kcal
Sprinting	405 kcal

make changes for life

The best way to lose weight is to try to adopt healthier eating habits that can be easily maintained as a way of life, not just when you are trying to slim down. Aim to lose no more than 2 lb per week to ensure you lose only your fat stores. People who go on crash diets lose lean muscle as well as fat and are much more likely to put the weight back on again soon afterward.

For women, the aim is to reduce daily calorie intake to around 1,500 kcal to achieve the desired weight loss, then to stick to around 2,000 per day thereafter to maintain this weight. Regular exercise will also make a huge difference: the more you can burn, the less you will need to diet.

the time to fit it into their hectic schedules. The easiest way to increase physical activity is by incorporating it into your daily routines, perhaps by walking or cycling instead of driving (particularly for short journeys), and taking up more active hobbies, such as gardening. You can also take small and simple steps, such as choosing to take the stairs instead of the elevator or escalator whenever possible.

As a general guide, adults should aim to undertake at least 30 minutes of moderate-intensity exercise, such as a brisk walk, five times a week. The 30 minutes do not have to be taken all at once: three sessions of 10 minutes are equally beneficial. Children and young people should be encouraged to get at least 60 minutes of moderate-intensity exercise every day.

improve your diet

For most of us, simply adopting a more balanced diet will reduce our calorie intake and lead to weight loss. Follow these simple recommendations:

- Eat more starchy foods, such as bread, potatoes, rice, and pasta. Assuming these replace the fattier foods you usually eat and you don't smother them with oil or butter, this will reduce the amount of fat and increase the amount of fiber in your diet. As a bonus, try to use wholegrain rice and whole-wheat pasta and flour, because the energy from these foods is released more slowly in the body, making you feel fuller for longer.

- Eat more fruit and vegetables, aiming for at least five portions of different fruits and vegetables (excluding potatoes) a day.

- As long as you don't add extra fat to fruit and vegetables in the form of cream, butter, or oil, these changes will help reduce your fat intake and increase the amount of fiber and vitamins you consume.

who said vegetables have to be dull?

Eat fewer sugary foods, such as cookies, cakes, and candy bars. This will also help reduce your fat intake. If you want something sweet, have some fresh or dried fruit instead.

Reducing the amount of fat in your diet means you will consume fewer calories overall. Choosing low-fat versions of dairy products such as skim milk and low-fat yogurt doesn't necessarily mean your food will be tasteless. Low-fat versions are available for most dairy products, including milk, cheese, cottage cheese, cream, sour cream, cream cheese, yogurt, and even butter.

simple steps to reduce your fat intake

Few of us have an iron will, so when you are trying to cut down make it easier on yourself by following these steps:

- Serve small portions to start with. You may feel satisfied when you have finished but, if you are still hungry, you can always go back for more.

- Once you have served your meal, put away any leftover food before you sit down to

eat. Avoid putting serving dishes heaping with food on the table because you will undoubtedly pick at them, even if you feel satisfied with what you have already eaten.

- Eat slowly and savor your food; you are more likely to feel full when you have finished. If you rush a meal, you may still feel hungry afterward.

- Make an effort with your meals—the food doesn't have to be low on taste as well as in calories. You will feel more satisfied with a meal you thoroughly enjoyed and will be less likely to look for comfort in a bag of potato chips or a candy bar.

- Plan your meals in advance to make sure you have all the ingredients you need. Rummaging around in the cupboards when you are hungry is unlikely to result in a healthy, balanced meal.

- Keep healthy, interesting snacks on hand for those times when you need something to pep you up. You don't need to succumb to a candy bar if there are other tempting treats on offer.

what is a vegetarian diet?

The Vegetarian Society (a charity based in Britain) defines a vegetarian as "Someone who lives on a diet of grains, legumes, nuts, seeds, vegetables, and fruits, with or without the use of dairy products and eggs. A vegetarian does not eat any meat, poultry, game, fish, shellfish, or by-products of slaughter." People may choose to follow a vegetarian diet for various reasons, including religious, health, ethical, and environmental.

Today, being a vegetarian, cooking for a vegetarian in your family, or choosing to have a couple of meat-free days a week is so easy now that supermarkets and health food stores offer a range of ingredients for making tasty and satisfying vegetarian dishes. Many people perceive vegetarian cooking as being time-consuming and featuring heavy stews of beans and lentils, nut loaves, and omelets. This book aims to dispel that myth. It provides more than 200 recipes to help you create simple, flavorful vegetarian feasts, with inspirational ideas for easy, nutritious dishes for breakfast and brunch, appetizers and snacks, main meals, soups and stews, salads and sides, breads and baking, and desserts. There's sure to be something here to please all tastes, vegetarian and nonvegetarian alike.

ingredients

For vegetarians, avoiding certain products can be tricky. For example, animal fat and ingredients such as gelatin may be used in manufactured foods. Rennet, which is extracted from the stomach lining of cows, is often used in making cheese. Also, some jars of curry paste may contain shrimp. In many cases, there are vegetarian alternatives to these ingredients, so it is advisable to take time to check the food labels.

cheese

Cheese is a good source of protein for vegetarians, but always check the label to ensure that it is suitable for vegetarians and doesn't contain animal rennet. Some hard cheeses are still made with animal rennet, although increasingly, cheese is being made with "microbial enzymes," widely used in the industry because they are a consistent and inexpensive coagulant.

The term "microbial enzyme" means that it is a synthetically developed coagulant, while the term "vegetable rennet" indicates one derived from a vegetable source. Soft cheeses, such as cream cheese and cottage cheese, are manufactured without rennet. Some cottage cheeses, however, may contain gelatin, which is derived from animal sources.

The following are cheeses suitable for vegetarians and useful to keep in the fridge:

goat cheese Made from goat milk, this cheese has a tangy flavor and can be either soft and creamy or hard, so can be suitable for shredding and grating.

feta This crumbly white Greek cheese is traditionally made from ewe milk or a mixture of ewe and goat milk, but is now sometimes made using cow milk. Salty in flavor, it is perfect in salads and with couscous or pasta.

mozzarella A fresh or unripened Italian cheese traditionally made from the milk of the water buffalo. A firm but creamy cheese, it tastes like fresh milk with a tangy edge. It melts well and has a unique stretchiness, making it the classic pizza-topping cheese.

cheddar Made from cow milk, a lot of Cheddar is now produced using vegetarian rennet. Sharp Cheddar has great flavor.

vegetarian pasta cheese This is an excellent vegetarian alternative to Parmesan cheese for use in risottos or pasta dishes.

taleggio From northern Italy, this mild-flavored, whole cow-milk cheese has a soft texture and a fruity, creamy character.

ricotta This soft Italian curd cheese is made from whey, which is drained and then lightly "cooked." It is creamy with a slightly grainy texture and delicate flavor. Relatively low in fat, it is used in many Italian dishes.

ensuring a balanced diet

A vegetarian diet can supply all the nutrients needed for health and vitality, and eating vegetarian diet can make it easier to achieve the desired "5 a day" consumption of fresh fruit and vegetables.

Although a vegetarian diet doesn't guarantee better health, any risk associated with eating red meat is obviously eliminated. Unless you are vegan, you will most likely be consuming other animal products, including eggs, cheese, butter, cream, and milk, but it is important to avoid the common trap of overcompensating for the lack of meat by consuming, in particular, large amounts of cheese, which is high in saturated fats that can lead to heart disease.

To get the most from our food, buy good-quality ingredients and avoid processed foods. Always purchase fruit, vegetables, and herbs in the freshest condition possible to gain the maximum nutritional benefits. There is a far greater choice now when it comes to buying organic, but it remains the more expensive option. It is always worthwhile purchasing organic free-range eggs, but beyond that you can choose which organic produce to buy according to your budget and what looks good on the day.

It can be useful to eat food from the following five food "groups."

• protein

Pulses (the dried seeds of peas, beans, or lentils) are excellent and inexpensive sources of protein and also contain minerals such as iron, zinc, and calcium.

Soy products, which include tofu and Quorn™, contain a form of "mycoprotein" and these are available ground, as burgers, fillets, and sausages.

Eggs, dairy products, nuts, and seeds contain zinc, valuable calcium, and iron, as well as protein.

• fruit and vegetables

Aim to eat at least five portions of fruit and vegetables a day, where one portion weighs about 3 ounces.

Choose a wide variety of different-colored fruits and vegetables to provide a balanced mixture of nutrients.

- carbohydrate-rich foods

Potatoes, pasta, rice, and pulses provide sustained energy from carbohydrates, as well as B vitamins and fiber. One-third of your food intake should be made up of carbohydrate, so try to eat one food from this group each meal.

- dairy products or alternatives

These are needed for protein and calcium. At least three portions should be eaten each day, where one portion is an 8-ounce glass of milk, a ½ cup of yogurt, or a piece of cheese weighing 1 ounce. Alternatives include rice milk, dried figs, nuts, green vegetables, and soy products, such as tofu.

- vitamins and minerals

Iron is vital for the maintenance of healthy red blood cells and to prevent anemia. Vegetarian sources include eggs, leafy green vegetables, whole-wheat bread, molasses, dried fruit (especially apricots), pulses, fortified breakfast cereals, peanut butter, and pumpkin, sesame, and sunflower seeds. Iron from vegetable sources is not as easily absorbed as that from animal sources. If eaten with food rich in vitamin C, the body's absorption of iron is enhanced. Drink fruit juice with your breakfast cereal or squeeze fresh lemon juice onto your green vegetables and salads.

Remember that the only sure-fire way of knowing what you are eating is to make your own meals. So, start cooking now and enjoy some fabulous and healthy vegetarian food.

recipes under 200 calories

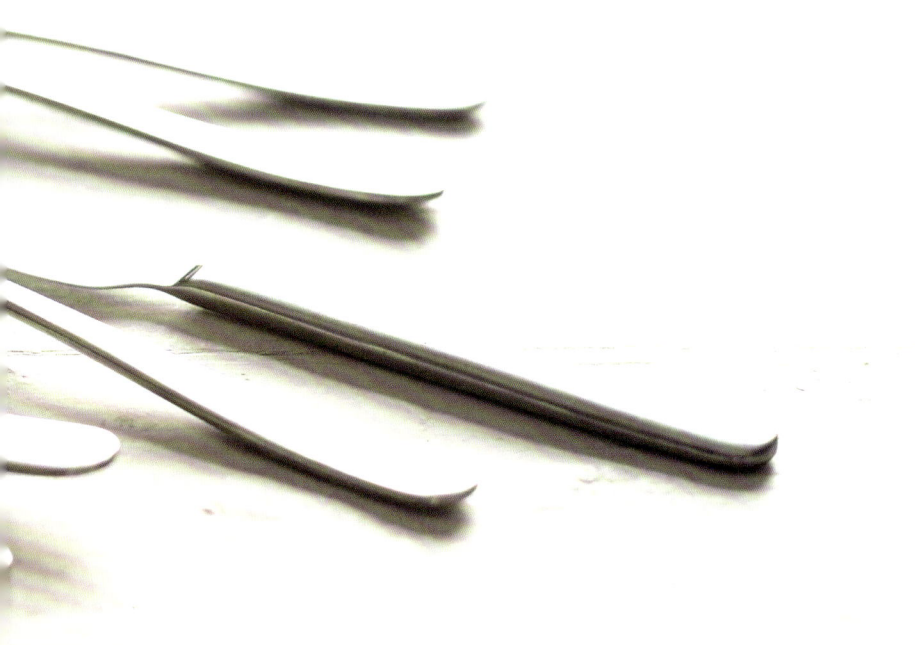

fruity summer smoothie

Calories per serving **103**
Makes **4 x 1¼ cup glasses**
Preparation time **2 minutes**

2 **peaches**, halved, stoned, and chopped
2 cups **strawberries**
2½ cups **raspberries**
1¾ cups **skim milk**
ice cubes

Put the peaches into a blender or food processor with the strawberries and raspberries and blend to a smooth puree, scraping the mixture down from the sides of the bowl if necessary.

Add the milk and blend the ingredients again until the mixture is smooth and frothy. Pour the mixture over the ice cubes in tall glasses.

For soy milk & mango shake, replace the peaches, strawberries, and raspberries with the flesh of 2 large ripe mangoes and the juice of 2 oranges. Puree as above, then pour in 1¾ cups soy milk. Blend and serve over ice cubes as above. **Calories per serving 138**

arugula, pear & pecorino salad

Calories per serving **195**
Serves **4**
Preparation time **10 minutes**

8 oz **arugula leaves**
2 **pears**
3 oz **pecorino cheese**, sliced into shavings

Dressing
1 teaspoon **Dijon mustard**
2 tablespoons **apple cider vinegar**
2 tablespoons **olive oil**
salt and **pepper**

Make the dressing by whisking the mustard, apple cider vinegar, and oil together. Season with salt and pepper.

Put the arugula into a large salad bowl. Finely slice the pears and add them to the arugula. Add the dressing to the salad and toss carefully to mix.

Layer most of the pecorino shavings through the arugula and pear salad, garnish with the remaining shavings, and serve.

For arugla, apple & balsamic salad, combine 8 oz arugula, 1 finely sliced green apple, and 3 oz pecorino cheese shavings in a large salad bowl. Whisk together 2 tablespoons aged balsamic vinegar with 3 tablespoons olive oil. Add the dressing to the salad, toss carefully to mix, and serve immediately.
Calories per serving 204

braised black cabbage & borlotti

Calories per serving **187**
Serves **4**
Preparation time **10 minutes**
Cooking time **30 minutes**

3 lb **cavolo nero (black cabbage)**
3 tablespoons **olive oil**
2 **garlic cloves**, thinly sliced
¼ teaspoon **dried red pepper flakes**
14-oz can **borlotti beans** (also called **cranberry beans**), rinsed and drained
salt

Remove the thick stalks of the cabbage by holding the stem with one hand and using the other hand to strip off the leaf. Discard the stalks. Cook the leaves in a saucepan of boiling water for 15 minutes, or until just tender, then drain thoroughly.

Heat the oil in a large skillet over low heat. Add the garlic, dried red pepper flakes, and borlotti beans and cook for 5 minutes, then stir in the cooked cabbage. Season with salt and cook, stirring, for 6 to 8 minutes, or until the cabbage has completely wilted and absorbed the flavors. Serve immediately.

For spinach with pine nuts, follow the recipe above from the second step onward, replacing the borlotti beans with ½ cup pine nuts. Use 1 lb baby spinach instead of the cabbage, add to the skillet raw, and cook, stirring, for 2 to 3 minutes, or until wilted. Stir a light grating of nutmeg into the cooked spinach before serving. **Calories per serving 204**

veggie stir-fry with bok choy

Calories per serving **186**
 (not including rice)
Serves **4**
Preparation time **10 minutes**
Cooking time **5 to 7 minutes**

8 small **pak choi**, about 1¼ lb in total
1 tablespoon **peanut oil**
2 **garlic cloves**, thinly sliced
1-inch piece of fresh **ginger root**, peeled and finely chopped
2 cups **snow peas**, sliced diagonally
7 oz **asparagus tips**, sliced in half lengthwise
7 oz **baby corn**, sliced in half lengthwise
¾ cup **podded edamame beans** or
2 cups **bean sprouts**
½ cup **sweet teriyaki sauce**

Cut the bok choy in half, or into thick slices if large, and put in a steamer basket. Lower into a shallow saucepan of boiling water so that the bok choy is not quite touching the water. Cover and steam for 2 to 3 minutes, or until tender. Alternatively, use a bamboo or electric steamer.

Heat a large wok or skillet over high heat until smoking hot, add the oil, garlic, and ginger and stir-fry for 30 seconds. Add the vegetables and stir continuously for 2 to 3 minutes, or until beginning to wilt.

Pour the sweet teriyaki sauce evenly over the vegetable mixture, toss to combine, and serve immediately with the steamed bok choy and some steamed rice, if liked.

For sweet chili vegetable stir-fry, heat the oil in the wok and stir-fry 1 thinly sliced onion with the garlic and ginger. Add 1 carrot, cut into thin matchsticks, and 2¾ cups sliced mushrooms and stir-fry for 2 minutes. Stir in 2 cups bean sprouts and 10 oz shredded spinach for a further minute, or until wilted. Stir in 1 cup sweet chili stir-fry sauce and serve immediately with the bok choy or cooked noodles.
Calories per serving 235

squash, kale & mixed bean soup

Calories per serving **182**
(not including garlic bread)
Serves **6**
Preparation time **15 minutes**
Cooking time **45 minutes**

1 tablespoon **olive oil**
1 **onion**, minced
2 **garlic cloves**, minced
1 teaspoon **smoked paprika**
1 lb **butternut squash**, halved, seeded, peeled, and diced
2 **small carrots**, peeled and diced
1 lb **tomatoes**, skinned (optional) and coarsely chopped
14-oz can **mixed beans**, rinsed and drained
4 cups hot **vegetable stock**
¾ cup **half-fat crème fraîche**
1½ cups **kale**, torn into bite-sized pieces
salt and **pepper**

Heat the oil in a saucepan over medium-low heat, add the onion, and fry gently for 5 minutes. Stir in the garlic and smoked paprika and cook briefly, then add the squash, carrots, tomatoes, and mixed beans.

Pour in the stock, season with salt and pepper, and bring to a boil, stirring frequently. Reduce the heat, cover, and simmer for 25 minutes, or until the vegetables are cooked and tender.

Stir in the crème fraîche, then add the kale, pressing it just beneath the surface of the stock. Cover and cook for 5 minutes, or until the kale has just wilted. Ladle into bowls and serve with warm garlic bread, if liked.

For cheesy squash, pepper & mixed bean soup, make as above, replacing the carrots with 1 cored, seeded, and diced red bell pepper. Pour in the stock, then add 2½ oz Parmesan cheese rinds and season. Cover and simmer for 25 minutes. Stir in the crème fraîche but omit the kale. Discard the Parmesan rinds, ladle the soup into bowls, and top with grated Parmesan. **Calories per serving 241**

cauliflower & chickpea curry

Calories per serving **180**
(**not including rice and raita**)
Serves **4**
Preparation time **10 minutes**
Cooking time **20 minutes**

1 tablespoon **peanut oil**
8 **scallions**, cut into 2-inch pieces
2 teaspoons **grated garlic**
2 teaspoons **ground ginger**
2 tablespoons **medium curry powder**
3 cups **cauliflower florets**
1 **red bell pepper**, cored, seeded, and diced
1 **yellow bell pepper**, cored, seeded, and diced
14-oz can **diced tomatoes**
14-oz can **chickpeas**, rinsed and drained
salt and **pepper**

Heat the oil in a large nonstick skillet over medium heat. Add the scallions and stir-fry for 2 to 3 minutes. Add the garlic, ginger, and curry powder and stir-fry for 20 to 30 seconds, or until fragrant. Now add the cauliflower florets and bell peppers and stir-fry for a further 2 to 3 minutes.

Stir in the tomatoes and bring to a boil. Cover, reduce the heat to medium, and simmer for 10 minutes, stirring occasionally. Add the chickpeas, season to taste, and bring back to a boil. Remove from the heat and serve immediately with steamed rice and mint raita, if liked.

For broccoli & black-eyed pea curry, follow the recipe above replacing the cauliflower with 3 cups broccoli florets, and the chickpeas with a 14-oz can black-eyed peas. **Calories per serving 179**

thai vegetable salad

Calories per serving **180**
Serves **4**
Preparation time **10 minutes, plus cooling**
Cooking time **2 minutes**

1¾ cups **cherry tomatoes**, quartered
1 **small cucumber**, thinly sliced
1 **green papaya** or **green mango**
1 large **red chile**, seeded and thinly sliced
1½ cups **bean sprouts**
4 **scallions**, trimmed and thinly sliced
small handful of **Thai basil leaves**
small handful of **mint leaves**
small handful of **cilantro leaves**
¼ cup **unsalted peanuts**, coarsely chopped

Chili dressing
2 tablespoons **sweet chili sauce**
2 tablespoons **light soy sauce**
2 tablespoons **lime juice**
2 tablespoons **lime marmalade**, warmed

Make the dressing. Put all the ingredients into a small saucepan and warm over low heat, stirring, until combined. Let cool.

Put the tomatoes, cucumber, papaya or mango, chile, bean sprouts, scallions, and herbs in a bowl. Add the dressing and toss well. Transfer to a platter. Scatter evenly with the peanuts and serve immediately.

For Thai salad wraps, serve the salad with large iceberg lettuce leaves. Spoon a little salad onto a leaf, roll up, and dip into the chili dressing. To cool the chili heat, omit the sweet chili sauce in the dressing.
Calories per serving 171

cannellini with sage & tomato

Calories per serving **179**
Serves **4**
Preparation time **10 to 15 minutes, plus soaking** (optional)
Cooking time **15 minutes** for canned beans; **45 minutes** for fresh; **1¾ hours** for dried

1½ cups shelled **fresh cannellini beans**, or 1 cup **dried cannellini beans**, soaked in cold water overnight, drained and rinsed, or 2 x 14-oz cans **cannellini beans**, rinsed and drained
1 **bay leaf** (optional)
2 **garlic cloves**, unpeeled, or 1 **garlic clove**, minced
2 teaspoons **olive oil**
1 **red onion**, thinly sliced
5 **sage leaves**, coarsely chopped
pinch of **dried red pepper flakes**
2 **tomatoes**, skinned and diced
salt
extra-virgin olive oil, for drizzling (optional)

Put the fresh beans, if using, into a saucepan, pour in enough cold water to cover by about 2 inches, and add the bay leaf, if using, and the unpeeled garlic cloves. Bring to a boil and skim off any scum that rises to the surface. Reduce the heat to a simmer and cook, uncovered, for 25 to 30 minutes, or until tender.

Drain, reserving the garlic cloves. If using presoaked dried beans, cook as for the fresh beans, but they will take about 1½ hours to become tender. The canned beans are ready to use.

Heat the oil in a large heavy skillet over low heat. Add the red onion, sage, and dried red pepper flakes and cook, stirring occasionally, for 10 minutes, or until the onion is softened. If you cooked the beans from scratch, squeeze the garlic flesh out of the skins into the pan. If using canned beans, simply add the minced garlic to the pan. Cook, stirring, for 1 minute, then add the beans and the tomatoes. Season with salt and cook, stirring, for 3 to 5 minutes. Serve drizzled with a little extra-virgin olive oil, if liked.

zucchini, feta & mint salad

Calories per serving **169**
Serves **4**
Preparation time **10 minutes**
Cooking time **10 minutes**

3 **green zucchini**
2 **yellow zucchini**
olive oil
small bunch of **mint**
1½ oz **feta cheese**
salt and **pepper**

Dressing
2 tablespoons **olive oil**
grated zest and juice of
  1 **lemon**

Slice the zucchini thinly lengthwise into long ribbons. Drizzle with oil and season with salt and pepper. Heat a ridged grill pan to very hot and grill the zucchini in batches until charred by the ridges in the grill pan on both sides, then transfer to a large salad bowl.

Make the dressing by whisking together the oil and the grated lemon zest and juice. Season to taste with salt and pepper.

Coarsely chop the mint, reserving some leaves for the garnish. Carefully mix together the zucchini, mint, and dressing. Transfer them to a large salad bowl, then crumble the feta evenly over the top, garnish with the remaining mint leaves, and serve.

For marinated zucchini salad, thinly slice 3 zucchini lengthwise and put them in a nonmetallic bowl with ½ seeded and sliced red chile, ¼ cup lemon juice, 1 crushed garlic clove, and ¼ cup olive oil. Season to taste with salt and pepper. Let the salad marinate, covered, for at least 1 hour. Coarsely chop a small bunch of mint, toss with the salad, and serve immediately. **Calories per serving 151**

vegetables with sweet chili sauce

Calories per serving **168**
Serves **4**
Preparation time **10 minutes**
Cooking time **5 minutes**

8 oz **cremini mushrooms**, trimmed and halved
2 tablespoons **cornstarch**
2 tablespoons **peanut oil**
1 tablespoon minced fresh **ginger root**
2 **garlic cloves**, thinly sliced
½ teaspoon **salt**
2 **red bell peppers**, cored, seeded, and cut into chunks
4 small **bok choy**, cut in half lengthwise
2 tablespoons **Chinese rice wine** or **dry sherry**
1 tablespoon **dark soy sauce**
1 tablespoon **sweet chili sauce**
4 **scallions**, thinly sliced

Place the mushrooms in a bowl with the cornstarch and toss to coat. Set aside.

Heat the oil in a wok over high heat until the oil starts to shimmer. Add the ginger, garlic, and salt and stir quickly, then add the mushrooms, red bell peppers, and bok choy and stir-fry for 2 to 3 minutes, or until just tender.

Stir in the rice wine, soy sauce, sweet chili sauce, and scallions and cook for 1 more minute, or until the sauce has thickened.

red cabbage slaw

Calories per serving **159** (not including bread)
Serves **4**
Preparation time **20 minutes**, plus marinating

- 1 lb **red cabbage**
- 1 **red onion**
- 1 **raw beet**
- 2 **carrots**
- 1 **fennel bulb**
- 2 tablespoons chopped **parsley** or **dill**
- ½ cup **raisins** or **golden raisins**

Dressing
- ½ cup **plain yogurt**
- 1 tablespoon **apple cider vinegar** or **white wine vinegar**
- 2 teaspoons **sweet German mustard** or **Dijon mustard**
- 1 teaspoon **liquid honey**
- 1 **garlic clove**, crushed
- **salt** and **pepper**

Trim the stalk off of the red cabbage and finely shred the cabbage. Cut the red onion in half and slice it thinly. Peel the beet and carrots and cut them both into thin matchsticks or grate coarsely. Halve the fennel bulb and shred it finely.

Put all the prepared vegetables, chopped parsley or dill, and raisins or golden raisins into a large salad bowl and toss them with your hands to combine well.

Make the dressing. Mix the yogurt with the vinegar, mustard, honey, crushed garlic, a pinch of salt, and plenty of pepper. Pour this dressing over the slaw, mix well, and let marinate for at least 1 hour. Serve the slaw with rye or sourdough bread.

For crunchy slaw with chili sauce, finely slice ½ lb white cabbage and ½ lb red cabbage. Cut 1 carrot into thin ribbons with a peeler and thinly slice 1 red onion and 1 fennel bulb. Make a dressing by mixing together 3 tablespoons sweet chili sauce, 1 tablespoon soy sauce, 1 tablespoon barbecue sauce, 2 tablespoons olive oil, and the juice of 2 limes. Toss the salad in the dressing and let stand for at least 30 minutes to let the flavors infuse before serving. **Calories per serving 151**

white bean soup provençal

Calories per serving **126**
  (not including bread)
Serves **6**
Preparation time **15 minutes, plus soaking**
Cooking time **20 minutes**

3 tablespoons **olive oil**
2 **garlic cloves**, crushed
1 small **red bell pepper**, cored, seeded, and chopped
1 **onion**, minced
1½ cups **diced tomatoes**
1 teaspoon finely chopped **thyme**
14-oz can **navy** or **cannellini beans**, drained and rinsed
2½ cups **vegetable stock**
2 tablespoons finely chopped **flat-leaf parsley**
salt and **pepper**

Heat the oil in a large heavy saucepan, add the garlic, red bell pepper, and onion and cook over medium heat for 5 minutes, or until softened.

Add the tomatoes and thyme and cook for 1 minute. Add the beans and pour in 2½ cups water and the stock. Bring to a boil, then reduce the heat, cover, and simmer for 15 minutes, or until the tomatoes have softened.

Scatter with the parsley and season with salt and pepper. Serve immediately in warmed soup bowls with fresh crusty bread.

For Spanish white bean soup, add 3½ oz diced chorizo when frying the onions, garlic, and red bell pepper. Stir in 1 teaspoon pimentón (Spanish smoked paprika) or 1 teaspoon mild chili powder. Cook for 1 minute until fragrant, then add the tomatoes and continue with the recipe as above. **Calories per serving 203**

trivandrum beet curry

Calories per serving **115**
Serves **4**
Preparation time **15 minutes**
Cooking time **25 to 30 minutes**

1 tablespoon **peanut oil**
1 teaspoon **black mustard seeds**
1 **onion**, chopped
2 **garlic cloves**, chopped
2 **fresh red chiles**, seeded and minced
8 **curry leaves**
1 teaspoon **ground turmeric**
1 teaspoon **cumin seeds**
1 **cinnamon stick**
13 oz **raw beets**, peeled and cut into matchsticks
1 cup **diced tomatoes**
½ cup **reduced-fat coconut milk**
juice of 1 **lime**
salt
chopped **cilantro leaves**, to garnish

Heat the oil in a wok or saucepan over medium heat. Add the mustard seeds and as soon as they begin to "pop" (after a few seconds), add the onion, garlic, and chiles. Cook for about 5 minutes, or until the onion is soft and translucent.

Add the remaining spices and the beets. Fry for a further 1 to 2 minutes, then add the tomatoes, 1 cup water, and a pinch of salt. Simmer everything for 15 to 20 minutes, stirring occasionally, until the beets are tender.

Stir in the coconut milk and simmer for a further 1 to 2 minutes, or until the sauce has thickened. Stir in the lime juice and check the seasoning. Garnish with chopped cilantro and serve immediately.

For spiced beet salad, thickly slice 1 ¼ lb cooked beets and arrange on a wide serving platter with 1 very thinly sliced red onion and a large handful of arugula leaves. Make a dressing by whisking 1 cup reduced-fat coconut milk with 1 tablespoon curry powder and ¼ cup each of very finely chopped cilantro and mint. Season to taste and drizzle evenly over the beet salad. Toss to mix well and serve. **Calories per serving 132**

malaysian spicy cauliflower

Calories per serving **118**
Serves **4**
Preparation time **10 minutes**
Cooking time **10 minutes**

2 tablespoons **peanut oil**
1 **red chile**, seeded and minced
1 **onion**, thickly sliced
2 **garlic cloves**, chopped
1 teaspoon **salt**
1 lb **cauliflower florets**, sliced

Heat the oil in a wok over high heat until the oil starts to shimmer. Add the chile, onion, and garlic and stir-fry for 1 minute.

Add the salt and cauliflower. Stir well to combine all the ingredients, then sprinkle with 3 tablespoons water, cover, and let steam for 3 to 4 minutes, or until tender.

For spicy cauliflower soup, start the recipe as above, adding ½ lb peeled and diced potatoes along with the cauliflower. Toss all of the ingredients together then pour in 4¼ cups vegetable stock. Simmer for 15 minutes, then blend until smooth. Serve with a drizzle of chili oil. **Calories per serving 186**

garden salad

Calories per serving **134**
Serves **4**
Preparation time **10 minutes**

½ **cucumber**
1¾ cups **cherry tomatoes**
8 oz **baby leaf mix**, such as **mizuna greens, baby chard, lollo rosso, purslane**, and **oakleaf lettuce**
1 **avocado**
½ cup **pitted black olives**

Dressing
1 teaspoon **Dijon mustard**
2 tablespoons **apple cider vinegar**
3 tablespoons **olive oil**
salt and **pepper**

Peel and slice the cucumber and halve the tomatoes Place them in a large salad bowl. Add the baby leaf mix and toss everything together gently to combine. Remove the seed from the avocado and peel and dice the flesh. Add the dice to the bowl along with the olives.

Make the dressing by whisking together the mustard, vinegar, and oil. Season to taste with salt and pepper.

Pour the dressing evenly over the salad, toss gently to combine, and serve.

chile kale

Calories per serving **95**
Serves **4**
Preparation time **8 minutes**
Cooking time **17 minutes**

1 tablespoon **olive oil**
1 **garlic clove**, crushed
1 large **white onion**, chopped
1 lb **curly kale**, stalks removed and leaves chopped
2 teaspoons **lime juice**
1 **red chile**, seeded and chopped
salt and **black pepper**

Heat the oil in a wok over medium heat. Add the garlic and onion and sauté for about 10 minutes, or until the onion is translucent.

Add the curly kale and stir-fry for another 5 minutes.

Stir in the lime juice and chile, season with salt and pepper to taste, and serve immediately.

For chile cabbage, replace the curly kale with 1 lb cabbage. Discard the stalks and tough outer leaves, then chop the leaves before frying with the garlic and onion and finishing as above. This dish also works well with collard greens. **Calories per serving 87**

strawberry & cucumber salad

Calories per serving **122**
Serves **4**
Preparation time **10 minutes**, **plus chilling**

1 large **cucumber**, halved lengthwise, seeded, and thinly sliced
1¾ cups **strawberries**, halved or quartered if large

Balsamic dressing
1 tablespoon **balsamic vinegar**
1 teaspoon **wholegrain mustard**
1 teaspoon **liquid honey**
3 tablespoons **olive oil**
salt and **pepper**

Put the cucumber slices and strawberry halves or quarters in a shallow bowl.

Add all the dressing ingredients to a jar, season to taste with salt and pepper, seal the lid securely, and shake well.

Pour the salad dressing evenly over the cucumber and strawberries. Toss gently, then cover and chill for 5 to 10 minutes before serving.

For cucumber & dill salad, prepare the cucumber as specified above, then put the slices in a colander set over a plate or in the sink. Scatter evenly with 2 teaspoons salt and let stand for 20 to 30 minutes, to allow the excess moisture to drain away. Rinse under cold running water, then drain thoroughly and transfer to a shallow serving dish. In a bowl, mix together ¼ cup thick Greek yogurt, 1 teaspoon white wine vinegar, and 2 tablespoons chopped dill. Season well with pepper. Pour evenly over the cucumber, toss gently to combine, and serve garnished with dill sprigs.
Calories per serving 51

peperonata

Calories per serving **143**
Serves **4**
Preparation time **10 minutes,** plus preparing the bell peppers
Cooking time **45 minutes**

2 large **red bell peppers**, broiled, skinned, cored, and seeded
2 large **yellow bell peppers**, broiled, skinned, cored, and seeded
2 teaspoons **olive oil**
1 small **onion**, minced
2 **garlic cloves**, minced
14-oz can **plum tomatoes**, coarsely chopped
6 large **basil leaves**, torn
extra-virgin olive oil, for drizzling (optional)
salt

Cut the bell peppers into wide strips and set aside.

Heat the oil in a heavy saucepan over low heat. Add the onion and cook, stirring occasionally, for 10 minutes. Add the garlic and cook, stirring, for 1 minute. Add the tomatoes, along with their juice, and the bell pepper strips. Season with salt and bring to a boil. Reduce the heat to a gentle simmer and cook, stirring occasionally, for 25 minutes.

Stir the basil into the pan and cook for 5 to 10 minutes, or until the sauce has reduced. Drizzle with extra-virgin olive oil before serving, if liked. Serve immediately as a side dish. Alternatively, serve cold as an antipasto.

For caper & lemon peperonata, follow the recipe as above, also adding 2 tablespoons capers and the grated zest of 1 lemon to the pan with the basil.
Calories per serving 144

marinated tofu & mushroom salad

Calories per serving **185**
Serves **4**
Preparation time **15 minutes**, plus marinating
Cooking time **5 minutes**

8 oz **firm tofu**
1 lb **mushrooms**, including **enoki, shiitake, wood ear,** and **oyster**

Marinade
1 **garlic clove**, minced
¾-inch piece of fresh **ginger root**, peeled and finely sliced
5 tablespoons **soy sauce**
1 tablespoon **mirin**
2 tablespoons **sweet chili sauce**
1½ tablespoons **sesame oil**
2 **star anise**

To garnish
5 **scallions**, finely sliced
2 tablespoons **sesame seeds**, toasted

Make the marinade. Mix the garlic and ginger with the soy sauce, mirin, sweet chili sauce, and oil. Add the star anise.

Put the tofu in a nonmetallic dish, pour the marinade evenly over the tofu, cover, and refrigerate for at least 2 hours, or overnight if possible.

Cut the mushrooms into bite-sized pieces and sauté in a little oil in a hot saucepan for 1 minute. Cut the marinated tofu into ¾-inch squares (reserve the marinade), mix with the mushrooms, and stir in the reserved marinade. Garnish with finely sliced scallions and sesame seeds and serve immediately.

For tofu & rice salad, cook 1 cup sushi rice according to the instructions on the package. While the rice is still warm, season it with ½ to ¾ cup rice seasoning vinegar. Cut 1 lb mixed mushrooms into bite-sized pieces and cook briefly, then mix through the rice with 1 carrot cut into julienne strips and a small bunch of finely sliced scallions. Mix the salad well, garnish with 3½ oz finely sliced deep-fried tofu and toasted sesame seeds and serve immediately. **Calories per serving 350**

spring vegetable salad

Calories per serving **131**
Serves **4**
Preparation time **10 minutes**
Cooking time **10 minutes**

1¼ cups **fresh** or **frozen peas**
7 oz **asparagus**, trimmed
3 cups **sugar snap peas**
2 **zucchini**
1 **fennel bulb**

Dressing
grated zest and juice of
  1 **lemon**
1 teaspoon **Dijon mustard**
1 teaspoon **liquid honey**
1 tablespoon chopped **flat-leaf parsley**
1 tablespoon **olive oil**

Put the peas, asparagus, and sugar snap peas in a saucepan of salted boiling water and simmer for about 3 minutes. Drain, then refresh under cold running water.

Cut the zucchini into long thin ribbons and thinly slice the fennel. Transfer all the vegetables to a large salad bowl and mix together.

Make the dressing by whisking together the lemon zest and juice, mustard, honey, flat-leaf parsley, and oil in another bowl. Toss the dressing through the vegetables and serve.

For beet dressing to serve with the spring vegetable salad, prepare the vegetables as above and set aside. Finely slice ½ red onion and 1 garlic clove. Heat 2 tablespoons olive oil in a saucepan over medium heat and gently cook the onion and garlic. Add 4 precooked beets and 6 roughly chopped sun-dried tomatoes and cook for a further 3 minutes. When the onions start to color deglaze the pan with 2 tablespoons balsamic vinegar. Cook for 1 minute, then add ½ cup vegetable stock. Reduce the stock by one-quarter, then let cool. Transfer the stock to a blender or food processor and blend until smooth. Season with salt and pepper and add up to 2 tablespoons cream, until the dressing reaches a drizzling consistency. Drizzle the dressing over the vegetables and serve. **Calories per serving 258**

arugula & parmesan salad

Calories per serving **139**
Serves **4 to 6, as a side dish**
Preparation time **5 minutes**

8 oz **arugula leaves**
¼ cup finely grated **Parmesan cheese**
1½ oz **Parmesan cheese**, sliced into shavings

Dressing
¼ cup **lemon juice**
2 tablespoons **olive oil**
½ teaspoon **Dijon mustard**
salt and **pepper**

Make the dressing by whisking the lemon juice, oil, and mustard together. Season to taste with salt and pepper.

Put the arugula into a large salad bowl, scatter with the grated Parmesan, and toss lightly to mix. Add the dressing and toss to combine. Garnish the salad with the Parmesan shavings and serve.

For arugula salad with chive dressing, blanch a bunch of chives in boiling water for 30 seconds until bright green. Refresh immediately in cold water. Squeeze out all the excess water, coarsely chop, and transfer to a blender. Add 3½ tablespoons mayonnaise, 1 tablespoon white wine vinegar, and salt and pepper to taste. Blend until smooth, adjusting the consistency with 1 tablespoon warm water if necessary. Mix 8 oz arugula with a thinly sliced fennel bulb, pour the dressing evenly over the mixture, toss together, and serve immediately. **Calories per serving 114**

okra, pea & tomato curry

Calories per serving **176**
Serves **4**
Preparation time **5 minutes**
Cooking time **about 20 minutes**

1 tablespoon **peanut oil**
6 to 8 **curry leaves**
2 teaspoons **black mustard seeds**
1 **onion**, minced
2 teaspoons **ground cumin**
1 teaspoon **ground coriander**
2 teaspoons **curry powder**
1 teaspoon **ground turmeric**
3 **garlic cloves**, minced
1 lb **okra**, cut on the diagonal into 1-inch pieces
1¼ cups **fresh** or **frozen peas**
2 ripe **plum tomatoes**, diced
salt and **pepper**
3 tablespoons grated **fresh coconut**, to serve

Heat the oil in a large nonstick wok or skillet over medium heat. Add the curry leaves, mustard seeds, and onion. Stir-fry for 3 to 4 minutes, or until fragrant and the onion is starting to soften, then add the cumin, ground coriander, curry powder, and turmeric. Stir-fry for a further 1 to 2 minutes until fragrant.

Add the garlic and okra, and increase the heat to high. Cook, stirring, for 2 to 3 minutes, then add the peas and tomatoes. Season to taste, cover, and reduce the heat to low. Cook gently for 10 to 12 minutes, stirring occasionally, until the okra is just tender. Remove from the heat and scatter with the grated coconut just before serving.

For spiced seeded pea & tomato pilaf, place 1½ cups basmati rice in a medium saucepan with 2 teaspoons dry-roasted cumin seeds, 1 tablespoon crushed dry-roasted coriander seeds, 2 teaspoons black mustard seeds, and 1¼ cups fresh or frozen peas, along with 3 peeled, seeded, and diced tomatoes. Add 2¾ cups hot vegetable stock, bring to a boil, and season to taste. Reduce the heat to low, cover the pan, and cook gently for 10 to 12 minutes, or until all the liquid has been absorbed. Remove from the heat and let stand, covered and undisturbed, for 10 to 15 minutes. Fluff up the grains with a fork to serve. **Calories per serving 341**

bok choy with chile & ginger

Calories per serving **48**
Serves **4**
Preparation time **5 minutes**
Cooking time **5 minutes**

1 tablespoon **peanut oil**
½ fresh **red chile**, sliced into rings
1 tablespoon chopped fresh **ginger root**
large pinch of **salt**
1 lb **bok choy**, leaves separated
¼ teaspoon **sesame oil**

Heat the peanut oil in a wok over high heat until the oil starts to shimmer. Add the chile, ginger root, and salt and stir-fry for 15 seconds.

Add the bok choy to the wok and stir-fry for 1 minute, then add ½ cup water and continue stirring until the bok choy is tender and the water has evaporated. Add the sesame oil, toss the leaves, and serve immediately.

shaved fennel & radish salad

Calories per serving **87**
Serves **4**
Preparation time **10 minutes**

2 **fennel bulbs**, about 1 lb 5 oz in total
10 oz **radishes**
2 tablespoons coarsely chopped **parsley**

Dressing
¼ cup **lemon juice**
2 tablespoons **olive oil**
salt and **pepper**

Slice the fennel and radishes as thinly as possible on a mandoline or with a knife, reserving the fennel fronds for the garnish. Toss together in a large salad bowl with the parsley.

Make the dressing by whisking together the lemon juice and oil. Season to taste with salt and pepper.

Add the dressing to the salad and toss gently to mix. Garnish with the reserved feathery fennel fronds and serve.

For pickled fennel salad, mix together 3 tablespoons apple cider vinegar, 1 tablespoon toasted cumin seeds, and 1¾ cups water in a small saucepan. Bring to a boil and season to taste with salt and pepper. Immediately pour the liquid over 1 lb 5 oz thinly sliced fennel and let cool. Drain the pickled fennel and serve as a side salad or as an accompaniment to grilled fish. **Calories per serving 40**

curried cabbage & carrot stir-fry

Calories per serving **84**
  (**not including rice**)
Serves **4**
Preparation time **10 minutes**
Cooking time **about
  15 minutes**

1 tablespoon **peanut oil**
4 **shallots**, minced
2 teaspoons finely grated
  peeled fresh **ginger root**
2 teaspoons finely grated
  garlic
2 fresh **long green chiles**,
  halved lengthwise
2 teaspoons **cumin seeds**
1 teaspoon **ground turmeric**
1 teaspoon **coriander seeds**,
  crushed
1 large **carrot**, coarsely grated
10 oz **green** or **white
  cabbage**, finely shredded
1 tablespoon **curry powder**
salt and **pepper**

Heat the oil in a large nonstick wok or skillet over low heat. Add the shallots, ginger, garlic, and chiles and stir-fry for 2 to 3 minutes, or until the shallots have softened. Add the cumin seeds, turmeric, and crushed coriander seeds and stir-fry for 1 minute.

Increase the heat to high and add the carrot and cabbage, tossing well to coat in the spice mixture. Add the curry powder and season to taste. Cover the pan and cook over medium-low heat for 10 minutes, stirring occasionally. Remove from the heat and serve immediately with steamed rice.

For speedy coconut, carrot & cabbage curry, heat 1 tablespoon peanut oil in a large wok and stir in 2 tablespoons medium curry paste, 2 chopped garlic cloves, and 1 sliced onion. Stir-fry for 3 to 4 minutes, or until softened. Chop 2 large carrots into ½-inch pieces and add to the onion mixture with 3¼ cups coarsely chopped cabbage, 1¼ cups vegetable stock, and 1 cup reduced-fat coconut milk. Bring to a boil, reduce the heat to medium, and cook for 12 to 15 minutes, or until the carrot pieces are tender. Remove from the heat and serve garnished with chopped cilantro.
Calories per serving 145

recipes under 300 calories

baked figs with goat cheese

Calories per serving **201**
Serves **4**
Preparation time **10 minutes**
Cooking time **10 to 12 minutes**

8 firm but ripe **fresh figs**
3 oz **soft goat cheese**
8 **mint leaves**
2 tablespoons **extra-virgin olive oil**
salt and **pepper**

Arugula salad
5 oz **arugula**
1 tablespoon **extra-virgin olive oil**
1 teaspoon **lemon juice**
salt and **pepper**

Cut a cross in the top of each fig without cutting right through the base. Put 1 teaspoonful of the goat cheese and a mint leaf in each fig. Transfer to a roasting pan, season with salt and pepper, and drizzle with the oil.

Bake in a preheated oven at 375°F for 10 to 12 minutes, or until the figs are soft and the cheese has melted.

Make the arugula salad. Put the arugula in a bowl. Whisk together the oil, lemon juice, salt, and pepper and drizzle it evenly over the arugula. Serve with the figs.

For figs stuffed with mozzarella & basil, replace the goat cheese with 4 oz sliced mozzarella and use basil leaves instead of the mint leaves. Continue the recipe as above. Serve with sprigs of watercress instead of the arugula. **Calories per serving 253**

spinach & pea frittata

Calories per serving **201**
  (not including salad)
Serves **4**
Preparation time **10 minutes**
Cooking time **25 minutes**

1 tablespoon **olive oil**
1 **onion**, thinly sliced
5 oz **baby spinach**
¾ cup shelled **fresh** or **frozen peas**
6 **eggs**
salt and **pepper**

Heat the oil in a heavy, 9-inch, ovenproof nonstick skillet over low heat. Add the onion and cook for 6 to 8 minutes, or until softened, then stir in the spinach and peas and cook for a further 2 minutes, or until any moisture released by the spinach has evaporated.

Beat the eggs in a bowl and season lightly with salt and pepper. Stir in the cooked vegetables, then pour the mixture into the pan and quickly arrange the vegetables so that they are evenly dispersed. Cook over low heat for about 8 to 10 minutes, or until all but the top of the frittata has set.

Transfer the pan to a preheated very hot broiler and cook about 4 inches from the heat source until the top is set but not colored. Give the pan a shake to loosen the frittata, then transfer to a plate to cool. Serve slightly warm or at room temperature, accompanied by a green salad, if liked.

For zucchini, pea & cheese frittata, follow the first step as above, but replace the spinach with 1 large zucchini, coarsely grated. Add ¼ cup freshly grated Parmesan cheese and 3½ oz mozzarella cheese, cubed, to the raw egg mixture with the vegetables and cook as above. **Calories per serving 312**

pickled vegetable salad

Calories per serving **209**
Serves **4**
Preparation time **20 minutes, plus cooling**
Cooking time **20 minutes**

8 small **shallots**
1 small **cauliflower**
1 **red bell pepper**
½ cup **white wine vinegar**
5 oz **green snap beans**
2½ cups **sugar snap peas**
3 oz **watercress**
¼ cup **olive oil**
salt and **pepper**

Trim the shallots and cut the cauliflower into small florets. Core and seed the bell pepper and cut the flesh into ¾-inch squares.

Put 4¼ cups cold water and the vinegar into a heavy saucepan, bring to a boil, and add the cauliflower, bell pepper, and shallots. Return the liquid to a boil and let boil for 2 minutes. Remove the saucepan from the heat and let the vegetables cool in the liquid.

Trim the beans and sugar snap peas and blanch in lightly salted boiling water. Refresh them in cold water and drain.

When the pickling liquid is cool, strain the vegetables and mix them with the beans, peas, and watercress in a large salad bowl. Dress with the olive oil, season to taste with salt and pepper, and serve.

For pickled cucumber & chile salad, cut 2 cucumbers in half lengthwise and remove the seeds by running a small teaspoon along the center. Slice the cucumber diagonally and place in a nonmetallic bowl. Add 1 tablespoon finely sliced pickled ginger, 1 seeded and finely sliced red chile, and 5 finely sliced scallions. Put a scant ½ cup superfine sugar, 5 tablespoons rice wine vinegar, and 1¾ cups cold water in a heavy saucepan and bring to a boil. Let cool, then pour the liquid over the cucumbers and let stand for at least 1 hour. The pickled cucumbers will keep for up to one week in a covered container in the refrigerator. **Calories per serving 123**

tomato & mozzarella salad

Calories per serving **212**
Serves **4**
Preparation time **15 minutes**

1 lb **ripe tomatoes**, preferably different types, such as **heritage**, **cherry**, and **plum**
about 3 tablespoons **olive oil**
2 tablespoons **aged balsamic vinegar**
small handful of **basil leaves**
5 oz **mini mozzarella balls**
salt and **pepper**

Cut half the tomatoes into thick slices and the other half into wedges. Arrange the slices on a large serving plate, slightly overlapping one another.

Put the tomato wedges in a bowl and drizzle with most of the olive oil and balsamic vinegar. Season to taste with salt and pepper. Mix gently and arrange carefully on top of the tomato slices.

Add the basil leaves and mozzarella balls to the tomato wedges. Drizzle the salad with more olive oil and balsamic vinegar, season to taste with salt and pepper, and serve.

For tomato & pasta salad, cook 8 oz fusilli or penne pasta until just tender. Refresh in cold water. Chop 1 lb tomatoes into chunks and stir them through the still-warm pasta, coat with olive oil, and season to taste with salt and pepper. Mix through a large handful of torn basil leaves, garnish with Parmesan cheese shavings, and serve. **Calories per serving 366**

smoked tofu & apricot sausages

Calories per serving **232**
  (not including fries
  and condiment)
Serves **4**
Preparation time **20 minutes**
Cooking time **10 minutes**

7½ oz **smoked tofu**
2 tablespoons **olive oil** or **vegetable oil**, plus a little extra for frying
1 large **onion**, coarsely chopped
2 **celery stalks**, coarsely chopped
½ cup **no-soak dried apricots**, coarsely chopped
½ cup **bread crumbs**
1 **egg**
1 tablespoon chopped **sage**
salt and **pepper**
flour, for dusting

Pat the tofu dry on paper towels and cut into chunks. Heat the oil in a skillet and fry the onion and celery for 5 minutes, or until softened. Add them to a food processor along with the tofu and apricots. Blend the ingredients to a chunky paste, scraping down the mixture from the sides of the bowl if necessary.

Pour the mixture into a large bowl and add the bread crumbs, egg, and sage. Season with salt and pepper and beat well until everything is evenly combined.

Divide the mixture into eight portions. Using lightly floured hands, shape each portion into a sausage shape, pressing the mixture together firmly.

Heat a little oil in a nonstick skillet and fry the sausages for about 5 minutes, or until they are golden. Serve with chunky fries and a spicy condiment, if liked.

For a spicy apple relish to serve with the sausages, peel and core 4 apples and cut them into chunks. Place in a saucepan with ½ cup hard cider, 1 stick cinnamon, 2 teaspoons light soft brown sugar, and ½ teaspoon dried red pepper flakes. Cover and cook over low heat until the apples have broken down into a pulp. Let cool before serving. **Calories per serving 78**

beet, spinach & orange salad

Calories per serving **221**
Serves **4**
Preparation time **20 minutes, plus cooling**
Cooking time **1 to 2 hours**

1 lb uncooked **beets**, preferably all of a similar size
2 **garlic cloves**, peeled and left whole
handful of **oregano leaves**
1 teaspoon **vegetable oil**
1 tablespoon **balsamic vinegar**
7 oz **baby spinach**
2 **oranges**, peeled, white pith removed, cut into segments
salt and **pepper**

Vinaigrette
1 tablespoon **balsamic vinegar**
1 teaspoon **Dijon mustard**
¼ cup **olive oil**
pinch of **sugar** (optional)

Place the whole beets into the center of a large piece of aluminum foil, along with the garlic and oregano. Season with pepper and drizzle with the vegetable oil and vinegar. Gather up the foil loosely and fold over at the top to seal. Place on a cookie sheet and bake in a preheated oven at 400°F for 1 to 2 hours (depending on how large the beets are), or until tender. Unwrap the foil parcel and let the beets cool before peeling and slicing them. Discard the garlic.

Make the vinaigrette. Whisk together the balsamic vinegar and mustard in a small bowl. Season with a little salt and pepper. Gradually add the olive oil, whisking constantly, until smooth and well combined. Taste and adjust the seasoning as needed, adding a pinch of sugar to reduce the acidity, if liked, bearing in mind the sweetness of the roasted beets. Whisk again until the sugar has dissolved. Alternatively, put all the vinaigrette ingredients in a jar with a lid, seal tightly, and shake vigorously until well combined.

Put the spinach in a large bowl and gently toss together with the beets and oranges. Drizzle the salad with the vinaigrette and season to taste with pepper.

For beet, spinach & goat cheese salad, prepare and roast the beets as above. Cool, peel, and slice, then add them to a salad bowl along with the spinach and vinaigrette dressing. Lightly toast 4 slices of ciabatta or French bread on both sides under a preheated broiler. Cut 3½ oz goat cheese into 4 slices and arrange on top of the toasted bread. Cook under the hot broiler for a few minutes, or until the cheese has melted, then serve on a bed of salad. **Calories per serving 407**

green curry with straw mushrooms

Calories per serving **225**
Serves **4**
Preparation time **10 minutes**
Cooking time **10 minutes**

1¼ cups **coconut milk**, plus extra for drizzling
2½ tablespoons **green curry paste**
1¼ cups **vegetable stock**
2 **eggplants**, coarsely chopped into large chunks
¼ cup **soft brown sugar**
4 teaspoons **soy sauce**
2 tablespoons finely chopped freshly peeled **ginger root**
14-oz can **straw mushrooms**, drained
1 small **green bell pepper**, cored, seeded, and thinly sliced
salt

Put most of the coconut milk and the curry paste in a saucepan over medium heat and stir well. Pour in the stock, then add the eggplant, sugar, soy sauce, ginger, and salt to taste.

Bring to a boil and cook, stirring, for 5 minutes. Add the mushrooms and green bell pepper, reduce the heat, and cook for 2 minutes, or until piping hot.

Serve in bowls, drizzled with a little extra coconut milk.

For vegetable korma, heat 1 tablespoon vegetable oil in a large saucepan, add 1 minced onion, 3 bruised cardamom pods, 2 teaspoons each of ground cumin and ground coriander, and ½ teaspoon turmeric and cook over low heat for 5 to 6 minutes, or until the onion is light golden. Add 1 seeded and chopped green chile, 1 crushed garlic clove, and a thumb-sized piece of fresh ginger root, peeled and grated, and cook for 1 minute, then add 14 oz prepared mixed vegetables, such as cauliflower, bell peppers, carrots, and zucchini, and cook for a further 5 minutes. Remove the pan from the heat and stir through 1 cup yogurt and 2 tablespoons ground almonds. Serve scattered with chopped cilantro.
Calories per serving 364

sage & goat cheese frittata

Calories per serving **232**
  (not including bread)
Serves **4**
Preparation time **10 minutes**
Cooking time **10 minutes**

2 tablespoons **butter**, plus extra if necessary
18 large **sage leaves**
2 oz **soft goat cheese**, crumbled
2 tablespoons **crème fraîche**
4 **eggs**
salt and **pepper**

Melt the butter in a nonstick skillet. As soon as it stops foaming, add the sage leaves and fry over medium-high heat, stirring, for 2 to 3 minutes, or until crisp and the butter turns golden brown. Take out 6 of the leaves and drain them on paper towels. Transfer the remaining leaves and butter to a bowl.

Beat the goat cheese and crème fraîche together in a separate bowl. Beat the eggs in another bowl, season with salt and pepper, then stir in the sage leaves with the butter.

Reheat the skillet, adding a little extra butter if necessary. Pour in the egg mixture and dot spoonfuls of the goat cheese mixture onto the eggs. Cook over medium heat for 4 to 5 minutes, or until the underside is set, then transfer to a preheated hot broiler to brown the top lightly. Let cool slightly, then gently slide the frittata onto a serving plate. Garnish with the reserved sage leaves and serve with crusty bread, if liked.

For spinach & goat cheese frittata, cook 6 oz baby spinach and 1 crushed garlic clove in the butter instead of the sage leaves for 2 minutes, or until the spinach has wilted. Stir into the beaten eggs at the second stage and continue with the recipe as above. **Calories per serving 240**

fennel & orange casserole

Calories per serving **232**
 (not including polenta)
Serves **4**
Preparation time **15 minutes**
Cooking time **about 50 minutes**

2 **fennel bulbs**, trimmed
¼ cup **extra-virgin olive oil**
1 **onion**, chopped
2 **garlic cloves**, crushed
2 teaspoons chopped **rosemary**
½ cup **Pernod**
14-oz can **diced tomatoes**
¼ teaspoon **saffron threads**
2 strips of **orange zest**
2 tablespoons chopped **fennel fronds**
salt and **pepper**

Cut the fennel lengthwise into slices ¼ inch thick. Heat half the oil in a Dutch oven, add the fennel slices in batches, and cook over medium heat for 3 to 4 minutes on each side until golden. Remove with a slotted spoon.

Heat the remaining oil in the Dutch oven, add the onion, garlic, rosemary, and salt and pepper and cook over low heat, stirring frequently, for 5 minutes. Add the Pernod, bring to a boil, and boil until reduced by half. Add the tomatoes, saffron, and orange zest and stir well. Arrange the fennel slices on top.

Bring the pot to a boil, then cover tightly with the lid and bake in a preheated oven at 350°F for 35 minutes, or until the fennel is tender. Stir in the fennel fronds and serve the casserole hot with some chargrilled polenta triangles, if liked.

For fennel gratin, prepare the fennel casserole as in the recipe above and transfer to a gratin dish. Combine 1¼ cups fresh white bread crumbs, ¼ cup grated Parmesan, and 2 tablespoons chopped parsley. Scatter it evenly onto the fennel mixture and bake, uncovered, for 35 minutes. **Calories per serving 384**

spicy eggplant curry

Calories per serving **231**
Serves **4**
Preparation time **15 minutes, plus cooling**
Cooking time **20 minutes**

1 teaspoon **cumin seeds**
4 teaspoons **coriander seeds**
1 teaspoon **cayenne pepper**
2 **green chiles**, seeded and sliced
½ teaspoon **turmeric**
4 **garlic cloves**, crushed
1-inch piece of **fresh ginger root**, peeled and grated
14-oz can **reduced-fat coconut milk**
1 tablespoon **tamarind paste**
1 large **eggplant**, thinly sliced lengthwise
salt and **pepper**
4 **plain mini naan breads**, to serve

Dry-fry the cumin and coriander seeds in a small, nonstick skillet for a few minutes until aromatic and toasted. Let cool, then crush together.

Mix together the crushed seeds, cayenne pepper, chiles, turmeric, garlic, ginger, and 1¼ cups warm water in a large saucepan and simmer for 10 minutes, or until thickened. Season with salt and pepper, then stir in the coconut milk and tamarind paste.

Arrange the eggplant slices on a foil-lined broiler rack and brush the tops with some of the curry sauce. Cook under a preheated hot broiler until golden.

Stir the broiled eggplant slices into the curry sauce. Serve hot with plain mini naan breads.

chermoula tofu & roasted veg

Calories per serving **241**
 (not including potatoes)
Serves **4**
Preparation time **15 minutes**
Cooking time **1 hour**

1 oz **cilantro**, finely chopped
3 **garlic cloves**, chopped
1 teaspoon **cumin seeds**, lightly crushed
finely grated zest of 1 **lemon**
½ teaspoon **dried red pepper flakes**
¼ cup **olive oil**
8 oz **tofu**
2 **red onions**, quartered
2 **zucchini**, thickly sliced
2 **red bell peppers**, seeded and sliced
2 **yellow bell peppers**, seeded and sliced
1 small **eggplant**, thickly sliced
salt

Mix the cilantro, garlic, cumin, lemon zest, and chiles together with 1 tablespoon of the oil and a little salt in a small bowl to make the chermoula.

Pat the tofu dry on paper towels and cut it in half. Cut each half horizontally into thin slices. Spread the chermoula generously over the slices.

Scatter the vegetables in a roasting pan and drizzle with the remaining oil. Bake in a preheated oven at 400°F for about 45 minutes, or until lightly browned, turning the ingredients once or twice during cooking.

Arrange the tofu slices over the vegetables, with the side spread with the chermoula uppermost, and bake for a further 10 to 15 minutes, or until the tofu is lightly colored. Serve with lightly buttered new potatoes, if liked.

stuffed mushrooms with tofu

Calories per serving **239**
Serves **4**
Preparation time **15 minutes**
Cooking time **18 to 20 minutes**

2½ cups hot **vegetable stock**
4 large **portobello mushrooms**, stalks removed
2 tablespoons **olive oil**, divided
½ cup minced **red onion**
2 tablespoons **pine nuts**
8 oz **tofu**, diced
½ teaspoon **cayenne pepper**
2 tablespoons chopped **basil**
½ cup finely grated **Parmesan cheese**
6 oz **baby spinach**
salt and **pepper**

Heat the stock in a pan over medium heat, add the mushrooms, poach for 2 to 3 minutes, then remove and drain on paper towels.

Heat a little of the oil in a skillet. Add the onion and fry gently until soft. Remove from the heat and let cool.

Dry-fry the pine nuts in a clean pan until golden-brown, remove from the heat, transfer to a bowl, then combine with the onion, tofu, cayenne pepper, basil, and the remaining oil. Season to taste with salt and pepper.

Sprinkle some grated Parmesan onto each mushroom, then stuff the onion mixture into the mushrooms. Transfer them to a broiler pan placed about 6 inches below a preheated medium broiler for 10 minutes, or until heated through and the cheese has melted.

Scatter the spinach onto 4 plates and arrange a hot mushroom on top of each (the heat from the broiled mushrooms will wilt the spinach).

For tofu & mushroom pasta, cook 10 oz pasta in boiling water according to the instructions on the package. Drain thoroughly. Meanwhile, slice 2 portobello mushrooms. Heat 1 tablespoon olive oil in a skillet and fry the mushrooms with ¼ cup chopped red onion. Add the mushrooms and onion to the pasta and add all the remaining ingredients above. Stir through 3 tablespoons double cream, warm gently, and serve. **Calories per serving 486**

summer vegetable soup

Calories per serving **248**
Serves **2**
Preparation time **10 minutes**
Cooking time **15 minutes**

1 teaspoon **olive oil**
½ **leek**, finely sliced
½ large **potato**, chopped
7 oz mixed summer vegetables, such as **peas**, **asparagus**, **fava beans**, and **zucchini**
1 tablespoon chopped **mint**
2 cups **vegetable stock** (see right for homemade)
1 tablespoon **crème fraîche**
salt (optional) and **black pepper**

Heat the oil in a medium saucepan, add the leek and potato, and fry for 2 to 3 minutes, or until softened.

Add the vegetables to the pan with the mint and stock and bring to a boil. Reduce the heat and simmer for 10 minutes.

Transfer the soup to a blender or food processor and process until smooth. Return to the pan with the crème fraîche and season with salt (if liked) and pepper. Heat through and serve.

For homemade vegetable stock, heat 1 tablespoon olive oil in a large saucepan. Add 1 chopped onion, 1 chopped carrot, 4 chopped celery stalks, and any available vegetable trimmings (such as celery trimmings, onion skins, and tomato skins) and fry for 2 to 3 minutes. Add 1 bouquet garni and season well with salt and pepper. Add 3½ pints water and bring to a boil. Reduce the heat and simmer gently for 1½ hours. Strain. This makes about 2½ pints of stock. **Calories per full amount 44**

malaysian coconut vegetables

Calories per serving **251**
Serves **4**
Preparation time **15 minutes, plus soaking**
Cooking time **20 minutes**

1¼ cups **broccoli florets**
1¼ cups **green snap beans**, cut into 1-inch pieces
1 **red bell pepper**, cored, seeded, and sliced
1 heaping cup thinly sliced **zucchini**

Coconut sauce
¼ cup **tamarind pulp**
½ cup **boiling water**
14 fl oz can **coconut milk**
2 teaspoons **Thai green curry paste**
1 teaspoon grated fresh **ginger root**
1 **onion**, cut into small cubes
½ teaspoon **ground turmeric**
salt

Make the coconut sauce. Put the tamarind pulp in a bowl. Add the measurement water and let soak for 30 minutes. Mash the tamarind in the water, then push through a sieve set over another bowl, squashing the tamarind so that you get as much of the pulp as possible; discard the stringy parts and any seeds.

Take 2 tablespoons of the cream from the top of the coconut milk and pour it into a wok or large skillet. Add the curry paste, ginger, onion, and turmeric and cook over very low heat, stirring, for 2 to 3 minutes. Stir in the rest of the coconut milk and the tamarind water. Bring to a boil, then reduce the heat to a simmer and add a pinch of salt.

Add the broccoli to the coconut sauce and cook for 5 minutes, then add the green beans and red bell pepper. Cook, stirring, for a further 5 minutes. Finally, stir in the zucchini and cook gently for 1 to 2 minutes, or until just tender. Serve immediately.

spring minestrone

Calories per serving **255**
  (not including bread
  or toast)
Serves **6**
Preparation time **15 minutes**
Cooking time **55 minutes**

2 tablespoons **olive oil**
1 **onion**, thinly sliced
2 **carrots**, peeled and diced
2 **celery stalks**, diced
2 **garlic cloves**, peeled
1 **potato**, peeled and diced
1 cup **peas** or **fava beans**,
  thawed if frozen
1 **zucchini**, diced
1¼ cups **green snap beans**,
  trimmed and cut into
  1½-inch pieces
¾ cup **plum tomatoes**,
  skinned and diced
2½ pints **vegetable stock**
¾ cup small **pasta shapes**
10 **basil leaves**, torn
salt and **pepper**

To serve
olive oil
grated **Parmesan cheese**

Heat the oil in a large heavy saucepan over low heat. Add the onion, carrots, celery, and garlic and cook, stirring occasionally, for 10 minutes. Add the potato, peas or fava beans, zucchini, and green snap beans and cook, stirring frequently, for 2 minutes. Add the tomatoes, season with salt and pepper, and cook for a further 2 minutes.

Pour in the stock and bring to a boil, then reduce the heat and simmer gently for 20 minutes, or until all the vegetables are very tender.

Add the pasta and basil to the soup and cook, stirring frequently, until the pasta is al dente. Season with salt and pepper to taste.

Ladle into bowls, drizzle with olive oil, and scatter each serving with the Parmesan. Serve with toasted country bread or Parmesan toast (see below).

For Parmesan toast to serve as an accompaniment, toast 6 slices of ciabatta on one side only under a preheated medium broiler. Brush the other side with 2 to 3 tablespoons olive oil and sprinkle with dried red pepper flakes and 2 tablespoons grated Parmesan cheese, then cook under the preheated broiler until golden and crisp. **Calories per serving 180**

chickpea & chile salad

Calories per serving **297**
Serves **4**
Preparation time **10 minutes, plus standing**

2 x 14-oz cans **chickpeas**, rinsed and drained
2 **plum tomatoes**, coarsely diced
4 **scallions**, thinly sliced
1 fresh **red chile**, seeded and thinly sliced
¼ cup coarsely chopped **cilantro leaves**
2 full-sized pieces of **pitta bread**, toasted and cut into thin fingers, to serve

Lemon dressing
2 tablespoons **lemon juice**
1 **garlic clove**, crushed
2 tablespoons **olive oil**
salt and **pepper**

Combine all the salad ingredients in a shallow bowl. Add all of the dressing ingredients to a jar, season to taste with salt and pepper, seal securely with the lid, and shake well. Pour the dressing onto the salad and toss everything well to coat.

Cover the salad and let stand at room temperature for about 10 minutes to allow the flavors to mingle. Serve with the toasted pitta bread fingers.

For white bean & sun-dried tomato salad, combine 2 x 14-oz cans cannellini beans, rinsed and drained, 4 oz sun-dried tomatoes in oil, drained and coarsely chopped, 1 tablespoon chopped and pitted black olives, 2 teaspoons rinsed and drained capers, and 2 teaspoons chopped thyme leaves. Add the lemon dressing, toss to coat, and let stand as above. Serve with toasted slices of ciabatta. **Calories per serving 454**

garlicky choy sum

Calories per serving **91**
Serves **4**
Preparation time **5 minutes**
Cooking time **5 minutes**

1 lb **choy sum**
2 tablespoons **peanut oil**
3 **garlic cloves**, sliced
1 teaspoon **salt**
2 tablespoons **Chinese rice wine** or **dry sherry**
1 teaspoon **sesame oil**

Trim 2 inches from the ends of the choy sum, then cut it into 2-inch pieces. Wash thoroughly.

Heat the oil in a wok over high heat until the oil starts to shimmer. Add the garlic and salt and stir-fry for 15 seconds, then add the choy sum and stir-fry for 1 minute.

Add the rice wine and ½ cup water and stir-fry for about 2 to 3 minutes, or until the choy sum is tender and most of the liquid has evaporated. Stir in the sesame oil and serve immediately.

For bok choy with water chestnuts & garlic, follow the recipe as above, replacing the choy sum with 1 lb bok choy, cut into 2-inch pieces, and 4 halved canned water chestnuts. **Calories per serving 97**

watermelon, fennel & feta salad

Calories per serving **266**
Serves **4**
Preparation time **10 minutes**
Cooking time **2 minutes**

2¼ cups **fresh** or **frozen shelled fava beans**
1 large **fennel bulb**
1¾ cups diced **watermelon**
4 oz **feta cheese**, crumbled
salt and **pepper**

Dressing
3 tablespoons **extra-virgin olive oil**
1 tablespoon **lemon juice**
1 teaspoon **liquid honey**
1 teaspoon **pomegranate syrup**

Cook the beans in a large saucepan of lightly salted boiling water for 2 minutes. Drain and immediately refresh under cold water. Pat dry with paper towels, then peel off and discard the tough outer skins. Put the beans in a bowl.

Trim the fennel bulb. Cut in half, then crosswise into wafer-thin slices. Add to the beans with the watermelon and feta cheese.

Whisk all the dressing ingredients together in a small bowl and season with salt and pepper. Pour evenly over the salad, toss well, and serve.

For fennel, orange & parsley salad, very thinly slice a large fennel bulb into a bowl and add ½ bunch of parsley, 2 tablespoons drained baby capers, and 1 peeled and segmented orange. Add the juice of ½ lemon, 1 tablespoon orange juice, and a good spoonful of extra-virgin olive oil. Season with salt and pepper and mix well to combine. **Calories per serving 63**

spicy apple & potato soup

Calories per serving **266**
Serves **4**
Preparation time **15 minutes**
Cooking time **30 minutes**

3½ tablespoons **butter**
1 small **onion**, chopped
2 **apples**, peeled, cored, and sliced
pinch of **cayenne pepper** (or to taste), plus extra for sprinkling
2½ cups **vegetable stock**
2 cups **potato** slices
1¼ cups **hot milk**
salt

Apple garnish
1 tablespoon **butter**
½ to 1 **apple**, peeled, cored, and diced

Melt the butter in a large heavy saucepan over medium heat. Add the onion and cook for 5 minutes, or until softened. Add the apples and cayenne pepper and cook, stirring, for a further 2 minutes.

Pour in the stock, then add the potatoes. Bring to a boil, then reduce the heat and simmer gently for 15 to 18 minutes, or until the apples and potatoes are very tender.

Blend the soup in batches in a blender or food processor until very smooth, then transfer to a clean saucepan. Reheat gently and stir in the hot milk. Taste and adjust the seasoning, if necessary.

Make the apple garnish, meanwhile. Melt the butter in a small skillet, add the diced apple, and cook over high heat until crisp.

Serve the soup in warmed bowls, garnishing each portion with some diced apple and a sprinkling of cayenne pepper.

For spicy apple & parsnip soup, fry the onion and apples as above, omitting the cayenne pepper. Add ½ teaspoon ground turmeric and 1 teaspoon ground coriander and stir through to coat the apple and onion mixture in the spices. Pour in 2½ cups vegetable stock, then add 2¼ cups diced parsnip instead of the sliced potatoes. Season with salt and black pepper. Continue the recipe as above. **Calories per serving 257**

italian broccoli & egg salad

Calories per serving **211**
  (not including bread)
Serves **4**
Preparation time **10 minutes**
Cooking time **8 minutes**

4 **eggs**
10-oz head of **broccoli**
2 small **leeks**, about 10 oz in total
sprigs of **tarragon**, to garnish (optional)

Dressing
¼ cup **lemon juice**
2 tablespoons **olive oil**
2 teaspoons **liquid honey**
1 tablespoon **capers**, rinsed and drained
2 tablespoons chopped **tarragon**
salt and **pepper**

Half-fill the base of a steamer with water, add the eggs, and bring to a boil. Cover with the steamer lid and simmer for 8 minutes, or until hard-cooked.

Meanwhile, cut the broccoli into florets and thickly slice the stems. Trim, slit, and wash the leeks and cut them into thick slices. Add the broccoli to the top of the steamer and cook for 3 minutes, then add the leeks and cook for a further 2 minutes.

Make the dressing by mixing together the lemon juice, oil, honey, capers, and tarragon in a salad bowl. Season to taste with salt and pepper.

Crack the eggs, cool them quickly under cold running water, and peel off the shells. Coarsely chop the eggs.

Add the broccoli and leeks to the dressing, toss together, and add the chopped eggs. Garnish with sprigs of tarragon and serve warm with thickly sliced whole-wheat bread, if liked.

eggplant, tomato & feta rolls

Calories per serving **270**
Serves **4**
Preparation time **15 minutes**
Cooking time **about 6 minutes**

2 **eggplants**
3 tablespoons **olive oil**
4 oz **feta cheese**, coarsely diced
12 **sun-dried tomatoes in oil**, drained
15 to 20 **basil leaves**
salt and **pepper**

Trim the ends off of the eggplants, then cut a thin slice lengthwise from either side of each; discard these slices, which should be mainly skin. Cut each eggplant lengthwise into 4 slices. Heat the broiler on the hottest setting or heat a ridged grill pan until very hot.

Brush both sides of the eggplant slices with the oil, then cook under the broiler or in the grill pan for 3 minutes on each side, or until browned and softened.

Lay the eggplant slices on a board and divide the feta, tomatoes, and basil leaves between them. Season well with salt and pepper.

Roll up each slice from the short end and secure with a toothpick. Arrange on serving plates and serve immediately, or cover and set aside in a cool place, but not the refrigerator, and serve at room temperature when required.

For zucchini & mozzarella rolls, use 3 to 4 large zucchini, then trim the ends and sides as for the eggplant. Cut each zucchini lengthwise into 3 slices, depending on their size, brush with oil, and cook under the broiler or in a grill pan as for the eggplant, until browned and softened. Spread the zucchini slices with 2 tablespoons red pesto, then top with 4 oz diced mozzarella cheese and the basil leaves. Roll up and serve as above. **Calories per serving 245**

fennel soup with olive gremolata

Calories per serving **218**
Serves **4**
Preparation time **20 minutes**
Cooking time **40 minutes**

⅓ cup **extra-virgin olive oil**
3 **scallions**, chopped
8 oz **fennel**, trimmed, cored and thinly sliced, reserving any green fronds for the gremolata and chopping them finely
1 **potato**, diced
finely grated zest and juice of 1 **lemon**
3¼ cups **vegetable stock**
salt and **pepper**

Gremolata
1 small **garlic clove**, minced
finely grated zest of 1 **lemon**
¼ cup chopped **parsley**
16 **black olives**, pitted and chopped

Heat the oil in a large saucepan, add the scallions, and cook for 5 to 10 minutes, or until beginning to soften. Add the fennel, potato, and lemon zest and cook for 5 minutes, or until the fennel begins to soften. Pour in the stock and bring to a boil. Turn down the heat, cover, and simmer for about 25 minutes, or until the ingredients are tender.

Make the gremolata. Mix together the garlic, lemon zest, chopped fennel fronds, and parsley, then stir in the chopped olives. Cover and chill.

Liquidize the soup and pass it through a sieve to remove any strings of fennel. The soup should not be too thick, so add more stock if necessary. Return it to the rinsed pan. Taste and season well with salt, pepper, and plenty of lemon juice. Pour into warmed bowls and scatter each serving with a portion of the gremolata.

For fennel & almond soup with orange & olive gremolata, add ½ cup blanched almonds to the pan with the onions. Complete the recipe as above, omitting the potato. Make the gremolata as above, replacing the lemon with the finely grated zest of 1 orange. **Calories per serving 293**

squash, carrot & mango tagine

Calories per serving **232**
(not including couscous)
Serves **4**
Preparation time **15 minutes**
Cooking time **35 to 40 minutes**

2 tablespoons **olive oil**
1 large **onion**, cut into large chunks
3 **garlic cloves**, minced
1¾-lb **butternut squash**, peeled, seeded, and cubed
2 small **carrots**, peeled and cut into thick batons
½-inch **cinnamon stick**
½ teaspoon **turmeric**
¼ teaspoon **cayenne pepper** (optional)
½ teaspoon **ground cumin**
1 teaspoon **paprika**
pinch of **saffron threads**
1 tablespoon **tomato paste**
3¼ cups hot **vegetable stock**
1 **mango**, peeled, seeded, and cut into 1-inch chunks
salt and **pepper**
2 tablespoons chopped **cilantro**, to garnish

Heat the oil in a large heavy saucepan over medium heat, add the onion, and cook for 5 minutes, or until beginning to soften. Add the garlic, squash, carrots, and spices and fry gently for a further 5 minutes.

Stir in the tomato paste, then pour in the stock and season with salt and pepper to taste. Cover and simmer gently for 20 to 25 minutes, or until the vegetables are tender. Stir in the mango and simmer gently for a further 5 minutes.

Ladle the tagine into serving bowls, scatter with cilantro, and serve with steamed couscous, if liked.

For spicy squash & carrot soup, make the tagine as above, adding an extra 1 cup vegetable stock. Once the vegetables are tender, place in a blender or food processor and blend until smooth. Ladle into bowls and serve scattered with the chopped cilantro. **Calories per serving 237**

stir-fried tofu with basil & chili sauce

Calories per serving **273**
Serves **4**
Preparation time **20 minutes**
Cooking time **6 minutes**

2 tablespoons **sunflower oil**, divided
11½ oz **firm tofu**, cubed
2-inch piece of fresh **ginger root**, shredded
2 **garlic cloves**, chopped
2¾ cups **broccoli**, chopped
8 oz **sugar snap peas**, trimmed
½ cup **vegetable stock**
2 tablespoons **sweet chili sauce**
1 tablespoon **light soy sauce**
1 tablespoon **dark soy sauce**
1 tablespoon **lime juice**
2 teaspoons **soft light brown sugar**
handful of **Thai basil leaves**

Heat half the oil in a wok or deep skillet until smoking, then add the tofu and stir-fry for 2 to 3 minutes, or until golden all over. Remove with a slotted spoon.

Add the remaining oil to the pan, add the ginger and garlic, and stir-fry for 10 seconds, then add the broccoli and sugar snap peas and stir-fry for 1 minute.

Return the tofu to the pan and add the stock, chili sauce, soy sauces, lime juice, and sugar. Cook for 1 minute, or until the vegetables are cooked but still crisp. Add the basil leaves and stir well.

For tofu & vegetables in oyster sauce, cook the tofu and vegetables as in the recipe above. Return the tofu to the pan and add ¼ cup water, cook for 1 minute, then add ⅓ cup oyster sauce and heat through for a further minute. Omit the basil and garnish with chopped fresh cilantro. **Calories per serving 244**

pumpkin soup with olive salsa

Calories per serving **235**
Serves **6**
Preparation time **20 minutes**
Cooking time **40 minutes**

¼ cup **olive oil**
1 large **onion**, chopped
2 **garlic cloves**, crushed
1 tablespoon chopped **sage**
2 lb peeled and cubed **pumpkin flesh**
14-oz can **cannellini** or **navy beans**, rinsed and drained
4¼ cups **vegetable stock**
salt and **pepper**

For the olive salsa
¾ cup **pitted black olives**
3 tablespoons **extra-virgin olive oil**
grated zest of **1 lemon**
2 tablespoons chopped **parsley**

Heat the oil in a saucepan, add the onion, garlic, and sage and cook over low heat, stirring frequently, for 5 minutes. Add the pumpkin and beans and stir well, then add the stock and a little salt and pepper.

Bring to a boil, then reduce the heat, cover, and simmer gently for 30 minutes, or until the pumpkin is tender. Transfer the soup to a blender or food processor and process until smooth. Return to the pan, adjust the seasoning, and heat through.

Meanwhile, make the salsa. Chop the olives and mix with the oil, lemon zest, parsley, and salt and pepper in a bowl.

Serve the soup in warmed bowls, topped with spoonfuls of the salsa.

For roasted butternut squash soup, use 2 lb of peeled butternut squash cubes instead of pumpkin. Toss the cubes of butternut squash with 1 tablespoon olive oil and roast in a preheated oven at 400°F for 30 minutes, or until golden and tender. Continue with the recipe as above, but cook the soup for just 15 minutes. **Calories per serving 291**

spicy lentils & chickpeas

Calories per serving **276**
 (**not including rice and yogurt**)
Serves **4**
Preparation time **15 minutes**
Cooking time **35 minutes**

1 tablespoon **peanut oil**
1 **onion**, minced
2 **garlic cloves**, thinly sliced
2 **celery stalks**, diced
1 **green bell pepper**, cored, seeded, and chopped
¾ cup **red split lentils**, rinsed
2 teaspoons **garam masala**
1 teaspoon **cumin seeds**
½ teaspoon **hot chili powder**
1 teaspoon **ground coriander**
2 tablespoons **tomato paste**
3¼ cups hot **vegetable stock**
14-oz can **chickpeas**, rinsed and drained
salt and **pepper**
2 tablespoons chopped **cilantro**, to garnish

Heat the oil in a heavy saucepan over medium heat, add the onion, garlic, celery, and green bell pepper and fry gently for 10 to 12 minutes, or until softened and beginning to color.

Stir in the lentils and spices and cook for 2 to 3 minutes, stirring frequently. Add the tomato paste, stock, and chickpeas and bring to a boil. Reduce the heat, cover, and simmer gently for about 20 minutes, or until the lentils collapse. Season with salt and pepper to taste.

Ladle into bowls and scatter with the cilantro. Serve immediately with boiled brown rice and cooling, spiced yogurt (see below), if liked.

For cooling, spiced yogurt to serve as an accompaniment, mix together 1 cup nonfat plain yogurt, 2 tablespoons lemon juice, and ½ teaspoon garam masala in a small bowl. Fold in ½ small, seeded and grated cucumber, then season with salt and pepper to taste. Scatter with 1 tablespoon chopped cilantro before serving. **Calories per serving 36**

mushroom stroganoff

Calories per serving **239**
Serves **4**
Preparation time **10 minutes**
Cooking time **10 minutes**

- 1 tablespoon **butter**
- 2 tablespoons **olive oil**
- 1 **onion**, thinly sliced
- 4 **garlic cloves**, minced
- 1 lb **cremino mushrooms**, sliced
- 2 tablespoons **wholegrain mustard**
- 1 cup **half-fat crème fraîche**
- **salt** and **pepper**
- 3 tablespoons chopped **parsley**, to garnish

Melt the butter with the oil in a large skillet, add the onion and garlic, and cook until soft and starting to brown.

Add the mushrooms to the pan and cook until soft and starting to brown. Stir in the mustard and crème fraîche and just heat through. Season to taste with salt and pepper, then serve immediately, garnished with the chopped parsley.

For mushroom soup with garlic croûtons, while the mushrooms are cooking, rub 2 thick slices of day-old white bread (crusts removed) with 2 peeled and halved garlic cloves. Cut the bread into cubes. Fry the cubes of bread in a little vegetable oil in a skillet, turning constantly, for 5 minutes, or until browned all over and crisp. Drain on paper towels. After adding the mustard and crème fraîche to the mushroom mixture as above, add 1¾ cups hot vegetable stock, then puree the mixture in a blender or food processor until smooth. Serve in warmed bowls, scattered with the croûtons and garnished with the chopped parsley. **Calories per serving 273**

grilled vegetable platter

Calories per serving **285** **(not including bread)**
Serves **4**
Preparation time **10 minutes**, **plus marinating**
Cooking time **20 minutes**

- 2 **zucchini**, cut lengthwise into slices ¼ inch thick
- 1 **eggplant**, cut lengthwise into slices ¼ inch thick
- 1 **yellow bell pepper**, cored, seeded, and cut into slices 1 inch thick
- 1 **red bell pepper**, cored, seeded, and cut into slices 1 inch thick
- ¼ cup **extra-virgin olive oil**, divided
- 2 **garlic cloves**, crushed
- large pinch of **dried red pepper flakes**
- handful of small **mint** and/or **basil leaves**
- **salt**

Toss all the prepared vegetables in 2 tablespoons of the oil until well coated.

Heat a ridged grill pan over high heat until smoking hot. Add the zucchini and eggplant in batches and cook for 2 to 3 minutes on each side. Transfer to a bowl and toss with the remaining oil, the garlic and dried red pepper flakes. Set aside.

Add the bell peppers in batches to the reheated grill pan and cook for 3 to 4 minutes on each side, then combine with the zucchini and eggplant. Season with salt and toss in the herbs.

Cover and let marinate at room temperature for 30 minutes. Serve with slices of country bread, if liked.

For grilled zucchini with lemon, mint & Parmesan, omit the bell peppers and eggplant and cut 4 large zucchini lengthwise into slices ¼ inch thick, toss with oil, and then cook as above. Transfer to a bowl and toss with the remaining oil, the garlic, and dried red pepper flakes as above, adding a handful of small mint leaves, torn, but not the basil. Let marinate as above, then serve with a generous topping of Parmesan cheese shavings and the finely grated zest of ½ lemon. **Calories per serving 326**

home-baked beans

Calories per serving **235 (not including toast)**
Serves **4**
Preparation time **10 minutes**
Cooking time **about 2 hours**

2 x 14-oz cans **cranberry beans**, rinsed and drained
1 **garlic clove**, crushed
1 **onion**, minced
2 cups **vegetable stock**
1¼ cups **passata** (sieved tomatoes)
2 tablespoons **molasses**
2 tablespoons **tomato paste**
2 tablespoons **soft dark brown sugar**
1 tablespoon **Dijon mustard**
1 tablespoon **red wine vinegar**
salt and **pepper**

Add all the ingredients to a Dutch oven with a little salt and pepper. Cover and bring slowly to a boil.

Bake in a preheated oven at 325°F for 1½ hours. Remove the lid and bake for a further 30 minutes, or until the sauce is syrupy. Serve with hot buttered toast, if liked.

For home-baked beans with baked potatoes, scrub 4 long russet potatoes, weighing about 7 oz each, then bake in a preheated oven at 400°F for about 1 hour, or until cooked through. Cut lengthwise in half and season with salt and pepper. Top each one with some beans and scatter with some shredded Cheddar cheese before serving. The home-baked beans are even better made a day ahead and heated through before serving.
Calories per serving 487

belgian endive & romaine salad

Calories per serving **288**
Serves **4**
Preparation time **10 minutes**

2 **Belgian endives, white and red** if possible, about 6 oz in total
3 **hearts of baby romaine lettuce**

Dressing
2 oz **Gorgonzola cheese**
1 tablespoon **Worcestershire sauce**
2 tablespoons **mayonnaise**
2 tablespoons **sour cream**
3 tablespoons **olive oil**
1 tablespoon **white wine vinegar**
2 tablespoons **lemon juice**
salt and **pepper**

Slice off the bottom of the Belgian endives and the lettuce hearts and carefully separate the individual leaves. Put the leaves in a large salad bowl.

Make the dressing by whisking together all the ingredients. Season to taste with salt and pepper.

Pour the dressing evenly over the leaves, toss briefly to coat, and serve.

For Gorgonzola, pecan & pear salad, prepare the salad leaves as above. Add ½ cup toasted pecans and 1 finely sliced pear to the Belgian endive and romaine lettuce leaves. Toss well to combine. Whisk the dressing ingredients as above, pour evenly over the salad, and toss gently to coat. Serve immediately. **Calories per serving 389**

carrot & cashew salad

Calories per serving **253**
Serves **4**
Preparation time **10 minutes**
Cooking time **6 to 10 minutes**

½ cup **unsalted cashews**
2 tablespoons **black mustard seeds**
1 lb **carrots**, peeled and coarsely grated
1 **red bell pepper**, cored, seeded, and thinly sliced
3 tablespoons chopped **chervil**
2 **scallions**, finely sliced

Dressing
2 tablespoons **avocado oil**
2 tablespoons **raspberry vinegar**
1 tablespoon **wholegrain mustard**
pinch of **sugar**
salt and **pepper**

Heat a nonstick skillet over medium-low heat and dry-fry the cashews for 5 to 8 minutes, stirring frequently, or until golden brown and toasted. Transfer to a small plate and let cool. Add the mustard seeds to the pan and dry-fry for 1 to 2 minutes, or until they start to pop.

Mix together the mustard seeds, carrots, red bell pepper, chervil, and scallions in a large bowl.

Whisk together all of the dressing ingredients in a small bowl, then pour evenly onto the grated carrot mixture. Toss thoroughly to coat and heap into serving bowls. Chop the cashews coarsely and scatter over the each portion. Serve immediately.

For carrot & celery root coleslaw, mix together 2¾ cups grated carrot and 1¾ cups coarsely grated celery root with the mustard seeds, chervil, scallions, and dressing, omitting the red bell pepper. Replace the cashews with ½ cup chopped walnuts and serve as above. **Calories per serving 253**

poached eggs & spinach

Calories per serving **291**
Serves **4**
Preparation time **5 minutes**
Cooking time **8 to 10 minutes**

4 strips of **cherry tomatoes** on the vine, about 6 tomatoes on each
2 tablespoons **balsamic syrup** or **glaze**
1 small bunch of **basil leaves**
1 tablespoon **distilled white vinegar**
4 large **eggs**
4 thick slices of **whole-wheat bread**
low-fat butter, to spread (optional)
3½ oz **baby spinach**
salt and **pepper**

Lay the cherry tomato vines in a baking dish, drizzle with the balsamic syrup or glaze, scatter with the basil leaves, and season with salt and pepper. Place in a preheated oven at 350°F for 8 to 10 minutes, or until the tomatoes begin to collapse.

Meanwhile, bring a large saucepan of water to a gentle simmer, add the vinegar, and stir with a large spoon to create a swirl. Carefully break 2 eggs into the water and cook for 3 minutes. Remove with a slotted spoon and keep warm. Repeat with the remaining two eggs.

Toast the whole-wheat bread and butter lightly, if liked.

Heap the spinach onto serving plates and top each plate with a poached egg. Arrange the vine tomatoes on the plates, drizzled with any cooking juices. Serve immediately with the whole-wheat toast, cut into fingers.

For spinach, egg & garden cress salad, gently lower the unshelled eggs into a saucepan of simmering water. Cook for 7 to 8 minutes, then cool quickly under cold running water. Shell the eggs and slice thickly. Arrange the egg slices onto the spinach and halved cherry tomatoes. Scatter with ¾ oz garden cress and serve with a little olive oil and balsamic syrup. **Calories per serving 241**

winter vegetable & beer broth

Calories per serving **237**
  (**not including bread**)
Serves **6**
Preparation time **20 minutes**
Cooking time **50 to 55 minutes**

¼ cup **olive oil**
1 **onion**, chopped
2 **garlic cloves**, crushed
1 tablespoon chopped **rosemary**
2 **carrots**, diced
2 cups diced **parsnips**
1¾ cups diced **rutabaga**
½ cup **pearl barley**
2½ cups **beer** or **lager**
4¼ cups **vegetable stock**
2 tablespoons chopped **parsley**
salt and **pepper**

Heat the oil in a large saucepan, add the onion, garlic, rosemary, carrots, parsnips, and rutabaga and cook over low heat, stirring frequently, for 10 minutes.

Stir in the pearl barley, beer or lager, stock, and salt and pepper and bring to a boil. Reduce the heat, cover, and simmer gently for 40 to 45 minutes, or until the barley and vegetables are tender. Stir in the parsley and adjust the seasoning. Serve in warmed bowls with crusty bread, if liked.

For vegetable & rice soup, omit the beer and increase the stock to 3 pints. Replace the pearl barley with an equal quantity of risotto rice. Use 2½ cups diced celery root instead of the parsnips. Continue the recipe as above. Serve the soup garnished with some more chopped parsley and cracked black pepper. **Calories per serving 195**

indian spiced pumpkin wedges

Calories per serving **292**
Serves **4**
Preparation time **15 minutes**, plus cooling
Cooking time **15 to 20 minutes**

2-lb **pumpkin** or **butternut squash**
1 teaspoon **cumin seeds**
1 teaspoon **coriander seeds**
2 **cardamom pods**
3 tablespoons **sunflower oil**
1 teaspoon **superfine sugar** or **mango chutney**

Coconut pesto
1 oz fresh **cilantro leaves**
1 **garlic clove**, crushed
1 **green chile**, seeded and chopped
pinch of **superfine sugar**
1 tablespoon **pistachios**, coarsely chopped
⅓ cup **coconut cream**
1 tablespoon **lime juice**
salt and **pepper**

Cut the pumpkin or butternut squash into thin wedges about ½ inch thick, discarding the seeds and fibers, and place in a large dish.

Heat a heavy skillet until hot, add the whole spices and dry-fry over medium heat, stirring, until browned. Let cool, then grind to a powder in a spice grinder or in a mortar using a pestle. Mix the ground spices with the oil and sugar or mango chutney in a small bowl, then add to the pumpkin wedges and toss well to coat.

Cook the pumpkin or squash wedges under a preheated hot broiler, or over a preheated hot gas barbecue or the hot coals of a charcoal barbecue, for 6 to 8 minutes on each side, or until charred and tender.

Meanwhile, make the pesto. Put the cilantro leaves, garlic, chile, sugar, and pistachio nuts in a food processor and blend until fairly finely ground. Season with salt and pepper. Add the coconut cream and lime juice and blend again. Transfer to a serving bowl. Serve the wedges hot with the coconut pesto.

For Indian-spiced sweet potato wedges, cook 4 scrubbed sweet potatoes, weighing 8 oz each, in a large saucepan of simmering water for 15 minutes, or until just tender, then drain. When cool enough to handle, slice into large wedges. Toss with the spice and oil mixture and broil or barbecue, as above, for about 6 minutes, turning frequently, until browned. Serve hot with the coconut pesto. **Calories per serving 419**

porridge with prune compote

Calories per serving **259**
Serves **8**
Preparation time **5 minutes**
Cooking time **about 20 minutes**

4¼ cups **skim milk**
1 teaspoon **vanilla extract**
pinch of **ground cinnamon**
pinch of **salt**
1¾ cups **porridge oats**
3 tablespoons **flaked almonds**, toasted

Compote
8 oz **ready-to-eat dried Agen prunes**
½ cup **apple juice**
1 small **cinnamon stick**
1 **clove**
1 tablespoon **liquid honey**
1 unpeeled **orange quarter**

Place all the compote ingredients in a small saucepan over medium heat. Simmer gently for 10 to 12 minutes, or until softened and slightly sticky. Let cool. (The compote can be prepared in advance and chilled.)

Put the milk, 2 cups water, vanilla extract, cinnamon, and salt in a large saucepan over medium heat and bring slowly to a boil. Stir in the oats, then reduce the heat and simmer gently, stirring occasionally, for 8 to 10 minutes, or until creamy and tender.

Spoon the porridge into warmed bowls, scatter with the almonds, and serve with the prune compote.

For sweet quinoa porridge with banana & dates, add 1½ cups quinoa to a saucepan with the milk, 1 tablespoon agave nectar or honey, and 2 to 3 cardamom pods. Simmer gently for 12 to 15 minutes, or until the quinoa is cooked and the desired consistency is reached. Serve in bowls topped with a dollop of nonfat plain yogurt, ½ cup chopped dates, and a freshly sliced banana. **Calories per serving 259**

recipes under 400 calories

baked tortillas with hummus

Calories per serving **312**
Serves **4**
Preparation time **5 minutes**
Cooking time **10 to 12 minutes**

4 small **soft flour tortillas**
1 tablespoon **olive oil**

Hummus
14-oz can **chickpeas**, rinsed and drained
1 **garlic clove**, chopped
¼ cup plain **Greek yogurt**
2 tablespoons **lemon juice**
1 small bunch fresh **cilantro**, chopped
salt and **pepper**
paprika, for dusting

Make the hummus first. Put the chickpeas in a bowl and mash with a fork to break them up. Add the garlic, yogurt, lemon juice, and cilantro and season with salt and pepper. Stir to combine. Alternatively, put all the ingredients, except the cilantro, in a blender or food processor and blend to a coarse puree. Add the cilantro and blend briefly until mixed through. Put the hummus in a serving bowl or dish and dust with a little paprika.

Cut each tortilla into 8 triangles, arrange on a cookie sheet, and brush with a little oil. Bake in a preheated oven at 400°F for 10 to 12 minutes, or until golden and crisp. Remove from the oven.

Serve the tortilla triangles with the hummus for dipping or spreading on top.

For baked tortillas with fava bean hummus,
cook 2½ cups frozen fava beans in boiling water for 4 to 5 minutes, or until tender. Drain, then mash or puree with the garlic, yogurt, lemon juice, salt and pepper, as above. Stir in 3 tablespoons chopped mint leaves, 1 seeded and chopped fresh green chili, and 1 teaspoon ground cumin instead of the cilantro.
Calories per serving 324

roasted summer vegetables

Calories per serving **399**
Serves **4**
Preparation time **15 minutes**
Cooking time **45 to 50 minutes**

1 **red bell pepper**, cored, seeded, and thickly sliced
1 **yellow bell pepper**, cored, seeded, and thickly sliced
1 **eggplant**, cut into chunks
2 **yellow** or **green zucchini**, cut into chunks
1 **red onion**, cut into wedges
6 **garlic cloves**
2 tablespoons **extra-virgin olive oil** or **canola oil**
4 to 5 fresh **thyme sprigs**
1 cup **yellow** and **red baby plum tomatoes**
1 cup **hazelnuts**
4 oz **arugula**
2 tablespoons **raspberry** or **balsamic vinegar**
salt and **pepper**
handful of **garden cress**, to garnish (optional)

Toss all the vegetables, except the tomatoes, in a large bowl along with the oil and garlic cloves. Season with a little salt and pepper and add the thyme. Transfer to a large roasting pan and place in a preheated oven at 375°F for 40 to 45 minutes, or until the vegetables are tender. Add the tomatoes and return to the oven for a further 5 minutes, or until the tomatoes are just softened and beginning to burst.

Add the hazelnuts to a small roasting pan, meanwhile, and place in the oven for about 10 to 12 minutes, or until golden and the skin is peeling away. Let cool, then remove the excess skin and crush lightly.

Toss the arugula gently with the mixture of roasted vegetables and heap onto large plates. Scatter with the crushed hazelnuts and drizzle with the vinegar. Scatter with garden cress, if using, and serve immediately.

For roasted vegetable pasta sauce, roast the vegetables as above, then add to a large saucepan with the rest of the vegetables, 2 cups passata (sieved tomatoes), and ½ cup vegetable stock. Bring to a boil, then reduce the heat and simmer gently for 20 minutes. Remove from the heat and use a hand-held blender to blend until smooth. Season with salt and pepper to taste and serve with hot pasta (5 oz per serving). Or, stir in an extra 1 cup vegetable stock to make soup. **Calories per serving sauce only 182 (with pasta 421)**

parsnip, sage & chestnut soup

Calories per serving **371**
Serves **4**
Preparation time **15 minutes**
Cooking time **50 minutes**

3 tablespoons ready-made or homemade **chili oil** (see below for homemade), plus extra for drizzling
40 **sage leaves**
1 **leek**, trimmed, cleaned, and chopped
1 lb **parsnips**, coarsely chopped
2½ pints **vegetable stock**
pinch of ground **cloves**
7-oz pack cooked peeled **chestnuts**
2 tablespoons **lemon juice**
crème fraîche, for topping
salt and **pepper**

Heat the chili oil in a large saucepan until a sage leaf sizzles and crisps in 15 to 20 seconds. Fry the remaining leaves in batches until crisp, lifting out with a slotted spoon onto a plate lined with paper towels. Set aside.

Add the leek and parsnips to the pan and fry gently for 10 minutes, or until softened. Add the stock and cloves and bring to a boil. Reduce the heat, cover, and cook very gently for 30 minutes, or until the vegetables are very soft. Stir in the chestnuts and cook for a further 5 minutes.

Blend the soup using a hand-held blender or in a food processor. Add the lemon juice and reheat gently, seasoning to taste with salt and pepper.

Ladle into warmed bowls, top with a little crème fraîche, and drizzle sparingly with extra chili oil. Serve scattered with the sage leaves.

For homemade chili oil, pour 1¼ cups olive oil into a saucepan. Add 6 whole dried chiles, 2 bay leaves, and 1 rosemary sprig and heat through gently for 3 minutes. Remove from the heat and let cool completely. Using a jug or funnel, pour into a thoroughly clean glass jar with a stopper or cork seal, adding the chiles and herbs. Cover and store in a cool place for one week before using. The chile flavor will become more intense during storage. Use as above, or in pasta and pizza recipes, or in any dish where you want to add a little heat. **Calories per tablespoon 117**

quick one-pot ratatouille

Calories per serving **301**
Serves **4**
Preparation time **10 minutes**
Cooking time **20 minutes**

½ cup **olive oil**
2 **onions**, chopped
1 **eggplant** cut into bite-sized cubes
2 large **zucchini**, cut into bite-sized pieces
1 **red bell pepper**, cored, seeded, and cut into bite-sized pieces
1 **yellow bell pepper**, cored, seeded, and cut into bite-sized pieces
2 **garlic cloves**, crushed
14-oz can **diced tomatoes**
¼ cup chopped fresh **parsley** or **basil**
salt and **pepper**

Heat the oil in a large saucepan until very hot. Add the onions, eggplant, zucchini, red and yellow bell peppers, and garlic, and cook, stirring constantly, for a few minutes until softened. Add the tomatoes, season with salt and pepper, and stir well.

Reduce the heat, cover the pan tightly, and simmer for 15 minutes, or until all the vegetables are cooked. Remove from the heat and stir in the chopped parsley or basil before serving.

roasted stuffed bell peppers

Calories per serving **398**
Serves **2**
Preparation time **10 minutes**
Cooking time **55 to 60 minutes**

4 large **red bell peppers**
2 **garlic cloves**, crushed
1 tablespoon chopped **thyme**, plus extra to garnish
4 **tomatoes**, halved
¼ cup **extra-virgin olive oil**
2 tablespoons **balsamic vinegar**
salt and **pepper**

Cut the red bell peppers in half lengthwise, then scoop out and discard the cores and seeds. Put the pepper halves, cut-side up, in a roasting pan lined with foil or in a ceramic dish. Divide the garlic and thyme between them and season with salt and pepper.

Place a tomato half into each pepper half and drizzle with the oil and vinegar. Roast in a preheated oven at 425°F for 55 to 60 minutes, or until the peppers are soft and charred.

For cheesy roasted peppers, use a mixture of green, yellow, and red bell peppers. After 45 minutes' cooking time, place a slice of mozzarella cheese (about 2 oz in total) on top of each pepper and return to the oven for the remaining 10 to 15 minutes. Serve with wedges of whole-wheat soda bread. **Calories per serving 458**

thai squash, tofu & pea curry

Calories per serving **308**
Serves **4**
Preparation time **15 minutes**
Cooking time **25 minutes**

1 tablespoon **peanut oil**
1 tablespoon **Thai red curry paste**
1 lb peeled and seeded **butternut squash cubes**
2 cups **vegetable stock**
1¾ cups **reduced-fat coconut milk**
6 **kaffir lime leaves**, bruised, plus extra shredded leaves to garnish
1¼ cups fresh or frozen **peas**
10 oz **firm tofu**, diced
2 tablespoons **light soy sauce**
juice of 1 **lime**

To garnish
cilantro leaves
fresh **red chile**, minced

Heat the oil in a wok or deep skillet, add the curry paste, and stir-fry over low heat for 1 minute. Add the butternut squash, stir-fry briefly, and then add the stock, coconut milk, and lime leaves.

Bring to a boil, then cover, reduce the heat, and simmer gently for 15 minutes, or until the squash is tender.

Stir in the peas, tofu, soy sauce, and lime juice and simmer for a further 5 minutes, or until the peas are cooked. Spoon into serving bowls and garnish with shredded lime leaves, chopped cilantro, and red chile.

For Thai green vegetable curry, use green curry paste instead of red curry paste. Replace the butternut squash with 1 sliced carrot, 1 sliced zucchini, and 1 cored, seeded, and sliced red bell pepper and follow the recipe above. **Calories per serving 298**

greek vegetable casserole

Calories per serving **310**
(not including bread)
Serves **4**
Preparation time **10 minutes**
Cooking time **25 minutes**

¼ cup **olive oil**, divided
1 **onion**, thinly sliced
3 **bell peppers** of mixed colors, cored, seeded, and sliced into rings
4 **garlic cloves**, crushed
4 **tomatoes**, chopped
7 oz **feta cheese**, cubed
1 teaspoon **dried oregano**
salt and **pepper**
chopped **flat-leaf parsley**, to garnish

Heat 3 tablespoons of the oil in a Dutch oven, add the onion, bell peppers, and garlic and cook until soft and starting to brown.

Add the tomatoes and cook for a few minutes until softened. Mix in the feta and oregano, season to taste with salt and pepper, and drizzle with the remaining oil.

Cover and cook in a preheated oven at 400°F for 15 minutes. Garnish with the parsley and serve with warmed crusty bread, if liked.

For Middle Eastern vegetable casserole, heat 1 tablespoon olive oil in a Dutch oven, add 1 red onion, cut into wedges, 3 sliced celery stalks, and 3 thinly sliced carrots. Cook until soft and starting to brown. Add 2 teaspoons harissa and cook, stirring, for 1 minute. Add about 1 ¼ lb trimmed and chopped eggplant, 2 large chopped tomatoes, and 1 cup water. Bring to a boil, then cover and cook in a preheated oven at 350°F for about 25 minutes. Stir in 2 large potatoes, peeled and thickly sliced, and cook for 15 minutes, or until tender but still firm. Serve hot, garnished with chopped cilantro. **Calories per serving 246**

curried cauliflower with chickpeas

Calories per serving **310**
  (not including chapatis)
Serves **4**
Preparation time **10 minutes**
Cooking time **20 minutes**

2 tablespoons **olive oil**
1 **onion**, chopped
2 **garlic cloves**, crushed
¼ cup **medium curry paste**
1 small **cauliflower**, divided into florets
1½ cups **vegetable stock**
4 **tomatoes**, roughly chopped
14-oz can **chickpeas**, rinsed and drained
2 tablespoons **mango chutney** (see right for homemade)
salt and **pepper**
¼ cup chopped **cilantro**, to garnish

Heat the oil in a saucepan, add the onion and garlic, and cook until the onion is soft and starting to brown. Stir in the curry paste, add the cauliflower and stock, and bring to a boil. Reduce the heat, cover tightly, and simmer for 10 minutes.

Add the tomatoes, chickpeas, and chutney and continue to cook, uncovered, for 10 minutes. Season to taste with salt and pepper. Garnish with cilantro and serve with rolled chapatis, if liked.

For homemade mango chutney, put the peeled, seeded, and sliced flesh of 6 ripe mangoes in a large saucepan with 1¼ cups white wine vinegar and cook over low heat for 10 minutes. Add 1 packed cup soft dark brown sugar, a 2-oz piece of fresh ginger root, peeled and finely chopped, 2 crushed garlic cloves, 2 teaspoons chili powder, and 1 teaspoon salt and bring to a boil, stirring constantly. Reduce the heat and simmer for 30 minutes, stirring occasionally. Ladle into a sterilized screw-top jar and seal securely. Store in the refrigerator and use within 1 month. **Calories for whole jar 449**

pumpkin with walnut pesto

Calories per serving **318**
Serves **4**
Preparation time **15 minutes**
Cooking time **20 to 25 minutes**

2-lb **pumpkin**
extra-virgin olive oil, for brushing
salt and **pepper**

Walnut pesto
½ cup **walnuts**, toasted
2 **scallions**, trimmed and chopped
1 large **garlic clove**, crushed
2 oz **arugula**, plus extra to serve
3 tablespoons **walnut oil**
3 tablespoons **extra-virgin olive oil**

Cut the pumpkin into 8 wedges. Remove the seeds and fiber but leave the skin on. Brush all over with olive oil, season with salt and pepper, and spread the wedges out on a large cookie sheet. Roast in a preheated oven at 425°F for 20 to 25 minutes, or until tender, turning halfway through.

Meanwhile, make the pesto. Put the walnuts, scallions, garlic, and arugula in a food processor and process until finely chopped. With the motor running, gradually drizzle in the oils. Season the pesto with salt and pepper.

Serve the pumpkin with the pesto and extra arugula.

For gnocchi with walnut pesto as an appetizer,
make the pesto as in the recipe above. Prepare and cook 13 oz fresh store-bought gnocchi according to the package instructions, or cook in boiling water until the gnocchi rise to the surface, then drain, transfer to a buttered serving dish, and top with the pesto.
Calories per serving **439**

cream of leek & pea soup

Calories per serving **322**
Serves **4**
Preparation time **15 minutes**
Cooking time **20 minutes**

2 tablespoons **olive oil**
12 oz **leeks**, slit, well washed, and thinly sliced
2½ cups freshly shelled or frozen **peas**
4 cups **vegetable stock**
small bunch of **mint**
5 oz **full-fat mascarpone cheese**
grated zest of 1 small **lemon**, divided
salt and **pepper**

To garnish (optional)
mint leaves
lemon zest curls

Heat the oil in a saucepan, add the leeks, toss in the oil to coat, then cover and fry gently for 10 minutes, stirring occasionally, until softened but not colored. Stir in the peas and cook briefly.

Pour the stock into the pan, add a little salt and pepper, then bring to a boil. Cover and simmer gently for 10 minutes. Ladle half of the soup into a blender or food processor, add all of the mint, and blend until smooth. Pour the puree back into the saucepan.

Mix the mascarpone with half of the lemon zest, reserving the rest for a garnish. Spoon half of the mixture into the soup, then reheat, stirring until the mascarpone has melted. Taste and adjust the seasoning if needed. Ladle the soup into warmed bowls, top with spoonfuls of the remaining mascarpone chese, and scatter with the remaining lemon zest. Garnish with mint leaves and lemon zest curls, if liked.

For cream of leek, pea & watercress soup, use 1¼ cups peas and add a coarsely chopped bunch of watercress. Simmer in 2½ cups of vegetable stock. Then, instead of adding the mascarpone, stir in ½ cup milk and ½ cup heavy cream, drizzling with a little extra cream at the end. **Calories per serving 327**

//
baked eggplant with tzatziki

Calories per serving **325**
Serves **4**
Preparation time **10 minutes, plus cooling**
Cooking time **50 minutes**

2 large **eggplants**, halved lengthwise
1 tablespoon **olive oil**, divided
heaping ½ cup **couscous**
boiling water
1 **onion**, minced
1 **garlic clove**, crushed
⅓ cup **ready-to-eat dried apricots**, chopped
⅓ cup **raisins**
grated zest and juice of 1 **lemon**
2 tablespoons chopped **mint**
2 tablespoons chopped **cilantro**
2 tablespoons freshly grated **Parmesan cheese**
4 portions of **flat bread**, to serve

Tzatziki
½ **cucumber**, finely chopped
2 **scallions**, sliced
1 cup plain **Greek yogurt**

Place the eggplant cut-side up on a cookie sheet and brush each with a little of the oil. Cook in a preheated oven at 400°F for 30 to 35 minutes, or until the flesh is tender, then remove (leaving the oven on) and let cool. When the eggplant is cool enough to handle, scoop out the flesh and roughly chop. Reserve the skins.

Place the couscous in a heatproof container, meanwhile. Add enough boiling water to cover the couscous by ½ inch, and cover the container with plastic wrap. Let stand for 5 minutes, then remove the wrap and run a fork through the couscous.

Heat the remaining oil in a nonstick skillet, add the onion and garlic, and fry for 3 minutes. Then stir through the apricots, raisins, lemon zest and juice, couscous, herbs, Parmesan, and eggplant flesh.

Spoon this mixture into the eggplant skins and return them to the oven for 10 minutes.

Mix together the tzatziki ingredients in a serving bowl and serve with the eggplant and flat bread.

For a spiced tomato sauce to serve with the eggplant instead of the tzatziki, heat 2 teaspoons olive oil in a saucepan and use it to cook 1 sliced onion for 5 minutes, or until beginning to soften. Add ½ teaspoon each of ground cinnamon, ground cumin, and ground ginger and cook for a further minute. Stir in a 14-oz can diced tomatoes and bring to a boil. Simmer, uncovered, for 20 minutes, then remove from the heat and season to taste with salt and harissa paste. Serve warm or at room temperature. **Calories per serving 53**

charred leek salad with hazelnuts

Calories per serving **341**
Serves **4**
Preparation time **10 minutes**
Cooking time **12 to 16 minutes**

1 lb **baby leeks**
1 to 2 tablespoons **hazelnut oil**
dash of **lemon juice**
1/3 cup blanched **hazelnuts**
2 **Little Gem** or **romaine lettuce hearts**
a few **mint sprigs**
1/2 oz **pecorino cheese**
20 **black olives**, to garnish

Dressing
1/4 cup **hazelnut oil**
2 tablespoons **extra-virgin olive oil**
2 teaspoons **sherry vinegar**
salt and **pepper**

Brush the leeks with the hazelnut oil. Cook, a few at a time, on a preheated hot, ridged grill pan or under a preheated hot broiler, turning frequently, for 6 to 8 minutes, or until evenly browned and cooked through. Toss with the lemon juice and season with salt and pepper. Let cool.

Heat a heavy skillet until hot meanwhile, add the hazelnuts, and cook over medium heat, stirring, for 3 to 4 minutes, or until browned. Let cool slightly, then chop coarsely. Separate the lettuce leaves and pull the mint leaves from the sprigs.

Arrange the leeks in serving bowls or on plates and top with the lettuce leaves, mint, and hazelnuts. Whisk all the dressing ingredients together in a small bowl, season with salt and pepper, and pour evely over the salad. Shave the pecorino onto the salad and serve garnished with the olives.

For charred asparagus salad with pine nuts,

replace the leeks with the same quantity of trimmed asparagus. Brush with extra-virgin olive oil instead of hazelnut oil, and cook and dress as in the recipe above. Toast pine nuts instead of hazelnuts, and use tarragon leaves in place of mint. For the dressing, use 1/4 cup extra-virgin olive oil, 2 tablespoons grapeseed oil, 2 teaspoons tarragon vinegar, and the grated zest of 1 lemon, reserving a few thin strips of zest. Shave a little Parmesan cheese over the salad and garnish with the reserved lemon zest strips. **Calories per serving 350**

walnut & blue cheese salad

Calories per serving **343**
Serves **4**
Preparation time **15 minutes**
Cooking time **5 minutes**

½ cup **walnut halves**
2 tablespoons **powdered sugar**
2 **Belgian endives**
2 oz **arugula**
1 **radicchio**, separated into leaves
4 oz **blue cheese**, such as **Roquefort**, crumbled

Dressing
1 teaspoon **Dijon mustard**
2 tablespoons **apple cider vinegar**
¼ cup **olive oil**

Put the walnuts in a plastic food bag with the powdered sugar and 1 tablespoon water and shake them until coated. Arrange the nuts on a cookie sheet and roast in a preheated oven at 350°F for 5 minutes, or until golden and crusted.

Separate the Belgian endive leaves and add them to a large salad bowl with the arugula and radicchio. Add the crumbled cheese and the walnuts and toss carefully.

Make the dressing by whisking together the mustard, vinegar, and oil. Drizzle the dressing evenly over the salad, toss lightly, and serve.

For grilled radicchio & Belgian endive salad, cut 2 Belgian endives in half and 2 radicchio into quarters. Dust well with 2 tablespoons powdered sugar and place on an oiled ridged grill pan over medium heat. Cook the Belgian endive and radicchio until golden and caramelized. Combine 3 tablespoons apple cider vinegar and ¼ cup olive oil with 2½ tablespoons golden raisins and heat them in a small saucepan. Pour evenly over the salad and toss to combine. Garnish with 3 tablespoons coarsely chopped parsley and 4 oz crumbled Gorgonzola cheese. **Calories per serving 273**

lentil moussaka

Calories per serving **304**
Serves **4**
Preparation time **10 minutes**
Cooking time **45 minutes, plus standing**

2/3 cup **dried brown or green lentils**, rinsed and drained
14-oz can **diced tomatoes**
2 **garlic cloves**, crushed
1/2 teaspoon **dried oregano**
pinch of **ground nutmeg**
1/2 cup **vegetable stock**
2 to 3 tablespoons **vegetable oil**
8 oz **eggplant**, sliced
1 **onion**, minced

Cheese topping
1 **egg**
5 oz **soft cheese**
pinch of **ground nutmeg**
salt and **pepper**

Put the lentils in a saucepan with the tomatoes, garlic, oregano, and nutmeg. Pour in the stock. Bring to a boil, then reduce the heat and simmer for 20 minutes, or until the lentils are tender but not mushy, topping off with extra stock as needed.

Meanwhile, heat the oil in a skillet over medium heat and lightly fry the eggplant and onion, until the onion is soft and the eggplant is golden on both sides.

Place the eggplant mixture and lentil mixture in alternating layers in a baking dish.

Make the topping. In a bowl, beat the egg, cheese, and nutmeg together to combine. Season generously with salt and pepper. Pour the topping evenly onto the moussaka and cook in a preheated oven at 400°F for 20 to 25 minutes. Remove from the oven and let stand for 5 minutes before serving with salad leaves.

For moussaka on baked potatoes, cook 4 scrubbed baking potatoes, weighing about 7 oz in total, in a preheated oven at 400°F for about 1 hour, or until tender, or cook in a microwave if preferred. Meanwhile, make the lentil mixture as above. Fry the eggplant and onion separately, then stir into the lentils when cooked. Spoon onto the slit potatoes, then top each one with a spoonful of soft cheese and scatter with some shredded Cheddar cheese. **Calories per serving 481**

corn & bell pepper frittata

Calories per serving **347** (**not including salad and bread**)
Serves **4**
Preparation time **10 minutes**
Cooking time **about 10 minutes**

2 tablespoons **olive oil**
4 **scallions**, thinly sliced
7-oz can **whole kernel corn**, drained
5 oz bottled **roasted red bell peppers** in oil, drained and cut into strips
4 **eggs**, lightly beaten
4 oz **sharp Cheddar cheese**, grated
small handful of **chives**, finely chopped
salt and **pepper**

Heat the oil in a skillet, add the scallions, corn, and red bell peppers and cook for 30 seconds.

Add the eggs, Cheddar, chives, and salt and pepper to taste, and cook over medium heat for 4 to 5 minutes, or until the bottom is set. Remove from the stove, place under a preheated broiler, and cook for 3 to 4 minutes, or until golden and set. Cut into wedges and serve immediately with a green salad and crusty bread, if liked.

For zucchini, bell pepper & Gruyère frittata, use 1 ½ cups finely chopped zucchini instead of the corn, 4 oz shredded Gruyère cheese in place of the Cheddar and substitute ¼ cup chopped mint leaves for the chives. **Calories per serving 305**

mushrooms à la grecque

Calories per serving **347**
Serves **4**
Preparation time **10 minutes, plus standing**
Cooking time **10 minutes**

½ cup **olive oil**, divided
2 large **onions**, sliced
3 **garlic cloves**, minced
1 lb 3½ oz **button mushrooms**, halved
8 **plum tomatoes**, roughly chopped or 14-oz can **diced tomatoes**
¾ cup **pitted black olives**
2 tablespoons **white wine vinegar**
salt and **pepper**
chopped **parsley**, to garnish

Heat 2 tablespoons of the oil in a large skillet, add the onions and garlic, and cook until soft and starting to brown. Add the mushrooms and tomatoes and cook, stirring gently, for 4 to 5 minutes. Remove from the heat.

Transfer the mushroom mixture to a serving dish and garnish with the olives.

Whisk the remaining oil with the vinegar in a small bowl, season to taste with salt and pepper, and drizzle evenly over the mushroom mixture. Garnish with the chopped parsley, cover, and let stand at room temperature for 30 minutes to allow the flavors to mingle before serving.

For mushroom pasta salad, prepare the mushroom mixture as above. Cook 7 oz dried pennette or farfalle in a large saucepan of salted boiling water according to the package instructions until al dente. Meanwhile, cook 4 oz green snap beans in a saucepan of salted boiling water until just tender. Drain the beans, refresh under cold running water, and drain again. Drain the pasta thoroughly and toss into the mushroom mixture along with the beans and 2 tablespoons torn basil leaves. Serve at room temperature. **Calories per serving 357**

fig, bean & toasted pecan salad

Calories per serving **352**
Serves **4**
Preparation time **5 minutes, plus cooling**
Cooking time **5 to 6 minutes**

1 cup **pecans**
7 oz **green snap beans**, trimmed
4 **fresh figs**, cut into quarters
3½ oz **arugula**
small handful of **mint leaves**
2 oz **Parmesan** or **pecorino cheese**

Dressing
3 tablespoons **walnut oil**
2 teaspoons **sherry vinegar**
1 teaspoon **vincotto**
salt and **pepper**

Heat a heavy skillet over medium heat, add the pecans, and dry-fry, stirring frequently, for 3 to 4 minutes, or until browned. Transfer to a small plate and let cool.

Cook the beans in a saucepan of lightly salted boiling water for 2 minutes. Drain, refresh under cold running water, and pat dry with paper towels. Put the beans in a bowl with the figs, pecans, arugula, and mint.

Whisk together all the dressing ingredients in a small bowl and season with salt and paper. If you can't find vincotto, use balsamic vinegar as an alternative. Pour evenly over the salad and toss well. Shave the Parmesan or pecorino cheese, scatter the salad with the shavings, and serve.

For mixed bean salad, combine 7 oz lightly cooked trimmed green snap beans with 2 x 14-oz cans drained mixed beans, 4 finely chopped scallions, 1 crushed garlic clove, and ¼ cup chopped mixed herbs, then dress with ¼ cup olive oil, the juice of ½ lemon, a pinch of superfine sugar, and salt and pepper to taste.
Calories per serving **259**

chickpea & bell pepper salad

Calories per serving **360**
(not including tzatziki)
Serves **4**
Preparation time **25 minutes**
Cooking time **35 minutes**

2 x 14-oz cans **chickpeas**
2 **red bell peppers**
1 **yellow bell pepper**
1 **red onion**
4 **plum tomatoes**, cut into wedges
olive oil
2 tablespoons **fennel seeds**
small bunch of **parsley**, chopped
salt and **pepper**
tzatziki (see below), to serve (optional)

Dressing
¼ cup **sherry vinegar**
3 tablespoons **olive oil**
1 **garlic clove**, crushed
½ teaspoon **ground cumin**

Rinse the chickpeas in cold water and let drain. Core and seed the peppers and cut the flesh into ¾-inch strips. Cut the onion in half and then cut each half into quarters, leaving the root attached so that the wedges remain intact.

Drizzle the bell peppers, onion, and tomatoes with olive oil and season with salt and pepper. Heat a ridged grill pan over high heat and cook the bell peppers for 2 minutes on each side. Place the bell peppers in a baking dish and cook the onion in the same way. Place the onion and tomatoes with the bell peppers, scatter with the fennel seeds, and cook in a preheated oven at 350°F for 20 minutes, or until done.

Meanwhile, make the dressing. Whisk together the vinegar and oil with the crushed garlic and cumin. Transfer the drained chickpeas to a large salad bowl and stir in the hot vegetables and chopped parsley. Season to taste with salt and pepper, drizzle with the dressing, and stir to combine. Serve with a dollop of tzatziki, if liked (see below).

For tzatziki to serve with the above salad, cut a cucumber in half lengthwise and scoop out the seeds using a spoon. Finely dice the flesh and mix it with 1 cup plain Greek yogurt, 1 crushed garlic clove, 1 tablespoon olive oil, 2 tablespoons chopped mint, and 1 tablespoon lemon juice. Season to taste with salt and pepper, cover, and leave in the refrigerator for at least 1 hour before serving. **Calories per serving 94**

thai red tofu & vegetable curry

Calories per serving **364**
 (not including rice)
Serves **4**
Preparation time **15 minutes**
Cooking time **25 to 30 minutes**

14½ oz **firm tofu**
1 tablespoon **canola oil**
2 tablespoons ready-made **Thai red curry paste**
1 to 2 fresh **green chiles**, sliced
7 fl oz canned **reduced-fat coconut milk**
1 cup **vegetable stock**
1 large **eggplant**, diced
12 **baby corn**
1½ cups **snow peas**
1¼ cup sliced **carrots**
4 oz **shiitake mushrooms**, halved
1 large **green bell pepper**, sliced
1 cup canned sliced **bamboo shoots**, drained
1 tablespoon **Thai fish sauce**
1 tablespoon **liquid honey**
2 **kaffir lime leaves**

To garnish
handful of **Thai basil leaves**
handful of **cashews**, toasted

Drain the tofu and pat it dry with paper towels before cutting it into 2-inch cubes.

Heat the oil in a wok over high heat until the oil starts to shimmer. Stir-fry the red curry paste and chiles for 1 minute, then stir in 2 tablespoons of the coconut milk (from the thicker part at the top of the can) and cook, stirring constantly, for 2 minutes.

Add the stock and bring to a boil. Add the eggplant, then bring the mixture back to a boil and simmer for about 5 minutes. Add the remaining vegetables and cook for another 5 to 10 minutes. Stir in the fish sauce, honey, lime leaves, and the remaining coconut milk and simmer for another 5 minutes, stirring occasionally. Add the tofu cubes and mix well.

Garnish with torn Thai basil leaves and toasted cashews. Serve with jasmine or sticky (glutinous) rice, if liked, which will absorb the wonderful aromatic sauce.

For one-pot tofu & vegetable noodles, use 1¾ cups reduced-fat coconut milk and increase the quantity of stock to 1½ cups. Add 5 oz cooked thick rice noodles along with the tofu and simmer for 1 minute. Serve garnished as above. **Calories per serving 499**

italian bean & artichoke salad

Calories per serving **367**
Serves **2**
Preparation time **10 minutes**

14-oz can **artichoke hearts**
1 small **red onion**, sliced
3-oz ball **mozzarella cheese**, cubed
14-oz can **cannellini beans**, rinsed and drained
3 oz **arugula**

Dressing
1 fresh **red chile**, minced
1 teaspoon **apple cider vinegar**
1 teaspoon **Dijon mustard**
1 teaspoon **superfine sugar**
1 tablespoon **olive oil**
1 tablespoon chopped fresh **mixed herbs** (such as **parsley**, **cilantro**, and **basil**)

Make the dressing. Whisk together the chile, vinegar, mustard, sugar, oil, and chopped herbs in a small bowl. Set aside.

Drain the artichoke hearts and mix them with the onion, mozzarella, and beans. Add the arugula and combine.

Stir the dressing through the salad and serve.

For quick bean & feta salad, cut 2 thick slices of bread into cubes. Brush them with 1 tablespoon olive oil, transfer to a roasting pan, and cook in a preheated oven at 400°F for 10 to 15 minutes, or until golden. Combine a 7-oz can mixed bean salad with 2 oz chopped feta cheese. Serve with chopped romaine lettuce and a handful of croutons. **Calories per serving 285**

lima bean & tomato soup

Calories per serving **379**
(not including bread)
Serves **4**
Preparation time **10 minutes**
Cooking time **20 minutes**

3 tablespoons **olive oil**
1 **onion**, minced
2 **celery stalks**, thinly sliced
2 **garlic cloves**, thinly sliced
2 x 14-oz cans **lima beans**, rinsed and drained
¼ cup **sun-dried tomato paste**
4 cups **vegetable stock**
1 tablespoon chopped **thyme** or **rosemary**, plus extra leaves to garnish
salt and **pepper**
Parmesan cheese shavings, to serve

Heat the oil in a saucepan over medium heat, add the onion, and fry for 3 minutes, or until softened. Add the celery and garlic and fry for 2 minutes.

Add the lima beans, sun-dried tomato paste, stock, rosemary or thyme, and season with salt and pepper. Bring to a boil, then reduce the heat, cover, and simmer gently for 15 minutes.

Ladle into warmed bowls and serve scattered with Parmesan shavings and extra thyme or rosemary leaves. This soup makes a light main course served with bread, if liked.

For spiced carrot & lentil soup, heat 2 tablespoons oil in a saucepan, add 1 chopped onion, 2 crushed garlic cloves, and 3 cups chopped carrots and fry for 10 minutes. Add a 14-oz can lentils, drained, 2 teaspoons ground coriander, 1 teaspoon ground cumin, and 1 tablespoon chopped thyme and fry for 1 minute. Stir in 2 pints vegetable stock, a 13-oz can diced tomatoes, and 2 teaspoons lemon juice and bring to a boil. Cover and simmer gently for 20 minutes. Put in a blender or food processor and blend until smooth, then return to the pan and warm through.
Calories per serving 240

lentil & feta salad

Calories per serving **386**
Serves **2 to 4**
Preparation time **15 minutes**
Cooking time **30 minutes**

1¼ cups **Puy lentils**
2 **carrots**, finely diced
2 **celery stalks**, finely diced
3½ oz **feta cheese**
2 tablespoons chopped **parsley**

Dressing
3 tablespoons **white wine vinegar**
2 teaspoons **Dijon mustard**
5 tablespoons **olive oil**
salt and **pepper**

Put the lentils in a saucepan, cover with cold water, and add a pinch of salt. Bring to a boil and cook for 20 to 25 minutes until just cooked but not mushy. Drain and refresh in cold water, then drain again and transfer to a large salad bowl.

Add the carrots and celery to the bowl with the lentils. Crumble in the feta and add the chopped parsley.

Make the dressing by whisking the vinegar, mustard, and oil. Add the dressing to the salad and stir well to combine. Season to taste with salt and pepper and serve immediately.

For lentil salad with poached eggs & asparagus, prepare the lentils as above. Blanch 1 lb asparagus, woody ends removed, then refresh and reserve. Slice the asparagus into 1¼-inch pieces, add it to the lentils with 2 tablespoons chopped parsley and 5 tablespoons olive oil and season with salt and pepper. Toss carefully to combine and transfer to serving plates. Place a poached egg onto of each salad and serve with 1 tablespoon of hollandaise sauce on top of the egg. **Calories per serving 492**

chickpea & herb salad

Calories per serving **389**
Serves **4**
Preparation time **10 minutes**, plus cooling
Cooking time **10 minutes**

½ cup **bulgur wheat**
¼ cup **olive oil**
1 tablespoon **lemon juice**
2 tablespoons chopped **flat-leaf parsley**
1 tablespoon chopped **mint**
14-oz can **chickpeas**, rinsed and drained
1 cup **cherry tomatoes**, halved
1 tablespoon minced **mild onion**
3½ oz **cucumber**
5 oz **feta cheese**, diced
salt and **pepper**

Put the bulgur wheat in a heatproof bowl and pour in enough boiling water just to cover. Set aside until the water has been absorbed. If you want to give a fluffier finish to the bulgur wheat, transfer it to a steamer and steam for 5 minutes. Spread on a plate to cool.

Mix together the olive oil, lemon juice, parsley, and mint in a large salad bowl. Season to taste with salt and pepper. Add the the chickpeas, tomatoes, onion, and bulgur wheat.

Dice the cucumber and add to the bowl. Mix well and add the feta, stirring lightly to avoid breaking up the cheese. Serve immediately.

For beet & chickpea salad, combine 5 oz baby chard with a 14-oz can rinsed and drained chickpeas and 7 oz precooked and diced beets in a large mixing bowl. Cut an orange in half and put the halves on a hot ridged grill pan until golden but not black. Squeeze the juice into a small bowl and add 1 teaspoon liquid honey and 3 tablespoons olive oil. Whisk together, then dress the salad lightly. Crumble 5 oz feta cheese and scatter it onto the salad to serve. **Calories per serving 304**

greek country salad with haloumi

Calories per serving **398**
Serves **4**
Preparation time **10 minutes**
Cooking time **2 minutes**

4 **vine-ripened tomatoes**, coarsely chopped
½ **onion**, sliced
1 **Lebanese cucumber (or small regular cucumber)**, thickly sliced
⅔ cup pitted **black Kalamata olives**
1 small **romaine lettuce**
8 oz **haloumi cheese**, sliced

Dressing
¼ cup **extra-virgin olive oil**
1 ½ tablespoons **red wine vinegar**
1 teaspoon **dried oregano**
salt and **pepper**

Put the tomatoes, onion, cucumber, and olives in a bowl. Tear the lettuce into pieces and add to the salad. Toss well and arrange on a large platter.

Whisk all the dressing ingredients together in a small bowl and season with salt and pepper. Drizzle a little over the salad.

Heat a heavy skillet until hot, add the haloumi slices, and cook for 1 minute on each side, or until they are charred and softened. Arrange on top of the salad, drizzle with the remaining dressing, and serve immediately.

For Greek salad with chunky croutons, replace the haloumi with 7 oz crumbled feta cheese. To make the croutons, cut thick slices of close-textured country bread, then cut these into large chunks. Heat a little olive oil in a skillet and fry the bread, turning occasionally, until crisp and golden. Add extra olive oil as needed. Cool, then toss into the salad, and serve immediately. **Calories per serving 410**

pepper & eggplant hummus

Calories per serving **343** (not including bread)
Serves **4**
Preparation time **10 minutes**, plus cooling
Cooking time **45 to 50 minutes**

- 1 **red bell pepper**, cored, seeded, and quartered
- 3 **garlic cloves**, unpeeled and lightly crushed
- 1 **eggplant**, cut into large chunks
- 1 tablespoon **chili oil**, plus extra to serve
- ½ tablespoon **fennel seeds** (optional)
- 14-oz can **chickpeas**, rinsed and drained
- 1 tablespoon **tahini**
- 1 teaspoon **sesame seeds**, lightly toasted
- **salt** and **pepper**

To serve
- 4 pieces **whole-wheat pitta bread**
- **olive oil spray**
- 1 teaspoon **paprika**

Arrange the bell pepper, garlic, and eggplant in a single layer in a large roasting pan. Drizzle with the chili oil and scatter with the fennel seeds, if using, and season with salt and pepper. Place in a preheated oven at 375°F for 35 to 40 minutes, or until softened and golden. Remove from the oven but do not turn it off.

Peel the skins from the garlic cloves and add to a blender or food processor with the roasted vegetables, three-quarters of the chickpeas, and the tahini. Blend until almost smooth, season to taste, and then spoon into a serving bowl. Cover with plastic wrap and let cool.

Cut the pitta bread into 1-inch strips and place in a large bowl. Spray with a little olive oil and toss with the paprika and a little salt until well coated. Arrange in a single layer on a cookie sheet. Toast in the oven for 10 to 12 minutes, or until crisp.

Sprinkle the hummus with the remaining chickpeas and the sesame seeds and drizzle with 1 to 2 tablespoons chili oil. Serve with the toasted pitta bread, if liked.

For roasted artichoke & bell pepper hummus,
replace the eggplant with a drained 14-oz can artichoke hearts in water. Roast in the oven with the bell peppers and garlic, as above, replacing the chili oil with 1 tablespoon lemon-infused oil. Omit the fennel seeds. Continue as above. **Calories per serving 356**

garlic & caramelized onion bhajis

Calories per bhaji **310**
Makes **6**
Preparation time **20 minutes**
Cooking time **5 minutes**

2 tablespoons **olive oil**, divided
1 **onion**, sliced
2 **garlic cloves**, sliced
1 teaspoon **cumin seeds**
2 tablespoons chopped **cilantro**
2¼ cups **chickpea/gram flour**
1 teaspoon **baking soda**
½ teaspoon **salt**

Heat half the oil in a nonstick skillet, add the onion, garlic, and cumin seeds and fry for 5 to 6 minutes, or until golden and softened. Stir in the cilantro.

Meanwhile, mix together the flour, baking soda, salt, and 1 cup water in a bowl. Set aside for 10 minutes, then stir it into the onion mixture.

Heat a little of the remaining oil in the skillet and add spoonfuls of the mixture, frying for 2 to 3 minutes, turning halfway through cooking. Cook the remaining mixture in the same way.

For an herb & yogurt chutney to serve with the bhajis, blend 2 tablespoons yogurt, a handful of mint leaves, and a handful of cilantro leaves in a blender or food processor with 1 tablespoon lemon juice until smooth. Stir into a bowl with another ¼ cup plain yogurt and season with salt. Cover and keep chilled until ready to serve the bhajis. **Calories per serving 24**

split pea & bell pepper patties

Calories per serving **312**
Serves **4**
Preparation time **15 minutes, plus chilling**
Cooking time **45 to 50 minutes**

3¼ cups **vegetable stock**
3 **garlic cloves**
1¼ cups **yellow split peas**
olive oil spray
2 **red bell peppers**, halved, cored, and seeded
1 **yellow bell pepper**, halved, cored, and seeded
1 **red onion**, quartered
1 tablespoon chopped **mint**, plus extra leaves to garnish
2 tablespoons **capers**, drained and chopped
flour, for dusting
salt and **pepper**

Tzatziki
½ **cucumber**, finely chopped
1 **garlic clove**, crushed
2 tablespoons chopped **mint**
1¼ cups **low-fat plain yogurt**

Bring the stock to a boil in a large saucepan. Peel and halve 1 of the garlic cloves, then add to the pan with the split peas and cook for 40 minutes, or until the split peas are tender. Season with salt and pepper and let cool slightly.

Meanwhile, lightly spray a roasting pan with oil. Place the remaining garlic cloves in the pan with the peppers and onion and cook in a preheated oven at 400°F for 20 minutes. Squeeze the roasted garlic cloves from their skins and chop with the roasted vegetables.

Mix together the split peas, roasted vegetables, mint, and capers in a large bowl. Flour your hands and shape the mixture into 12 patties. Chill until ready to cook.

For the tzatziki, mix the ingredients together, cover, and chill in the refrigerator for 30 minutes before serving.

Heat a skillet and spray with oil. Cook the patties, in batches if necessary, for 2 minutes on each side. Serve 3 patties per person, hot or cold, garnished with mint leaves, along with a small bowl of tzatziki.

sweet potatoes & tomato salsa

Calories per serving **384**
Serves **2**
Preparation time **5 minutes**
Cooking time **45 minutes**

2 large **sweet potatoes**, each about 9 oz
2 oz **Emmental** or **Cheddar cheese**, shredded
salt

Tomato salsa
2 large **tomatoes**, diced
½ small **red onion**, minced
1 **celery stalk**, minced
small handful of **cilantro**, chopped
2 tablespoons **lime juice**
2 teaspoons **superfine sugar**

Scrub the potatoes and put them in a small roasting pan. Prick with a fork and scatter with a little salt. Bake in a preheated oven at 400°F for 45 minutes, or until tender. (If you do not have the time to bake the sweet potatoes, they can be microwaved like ordinary ones, though this way you will lose the wonderful crispy baked flavor. Prick them with a fork and cook on the highest setting for 15 to 20 minutes, or according to the microwave manufacturer's instructions.)

Meanwhile, make the salsa. Mix the tomatoes in a bowl with the onion, celery, cilantro, lime juice, and sugar.

Halve the potatoes and fluff up the flesh with a fork. Sprinkle with cheese and top with salsa.

For sweet potatoes with cilantro dressing, bake the potatoes as above. Omit the tomato salsa and cheese. Make a dressing by combining ½ cup half-fat crème fraîche, 4 sliced scallions, a handful of chopped cilantro, and the zest and juice of 1 lime. Put the halved potatoes on serving plates and fluff up the flesh. Serve with a generous dollop of dressing. **Calories per serving 342**

recipes under 500 calories

baked sweet potatoes

Calories per serving **405**
Serves **4**
Preparation time **5 minutes**
Cooking time **45 to 50 minutes**

4 **sweet potatoes**, about 8 oz each, scrubbed
1 cup **sour cream**
2 **scallions**, trimmed and minced
1 tablespoon chopped **chives**
3½ tablespoons **butter**
salt and **pepper**

Put the potatoes in a roasting pan and roast in a preheated oven at 425°F for 45 to 50 minutes, or until cooked through.

Combine the sour cream, scallions, chives, and salt and pepper in a bowl.

Cut the baked potatoes in half lengthwise, add some butter, and spoon the sour-cream mixture on top. Serve immediately.

For crispy sweet potato skins, let the baked sweet potatoes cool, cut into wedges, and scoop out some of the soft potato (and use elsewhere), leaving a good lining inside the skin. Deep-fry in hot oil for 4 to 5 minutes, or until crisp. Serve with a dip of sour cream and chopped chives. **Calories per serving 444**

grilled vegetable & haloumi salad

Calories per serving **416**
Serves **4**
Preparation time **15 minutes**
Cooking time **25 minutes**

12 **cherry tomatoes** on the vine
4 **portobello mushrooms**
olive oil
2 **zucchini**, cut into batons about 1½ x ¾ inches
1 lb fresh **asparagus**, trimmed
8 oz **haloumi cheese**, cut into ¼-inch slices
salt and **pepper**

Dressing
2 tablespoons **olive oil**
2 tablespoons **balsamic vinegar**

Put the tomatoes and mushrooms in a roasting pan, drizzle with about 2 tablespoons oil, season with salt and pepper, and cook in a preheated oven at 350°F for 10 minutes.

Put the zucchini and asparagus in a large bowl, meanwhile. Drizzle with olive oil and a pinch of salt and pepper. Heat a ridged grill pan over high heat, and grill the asparagus and zucchini until starting to color. Transfer the asparagus and zucchini to the oven with the tomatoes and mushrooms and cook for 6 to 8 minutes.

Use a sheet of paper towel to wipe the grill pan clean. Pat the cheese slices dry with paper towels. Heat 1 teaspoon olive oil in the pan over medium heat. Grill the haloumi, turning once (use a spatula to loosen the cheese first), for about 4 minutes, or until lightly golden with char marks on both sides. Make the dressing by whisking together the oil and vinegar. Stack the grilled vegetables and mushrooms on 4 warmed plates, dividing the ingredients evenly. Top with slices of cheese, spoon over the dressing, and serve immediately.

For watermelon & haloumi cheese, cut 8 oz haloumi cheese into thin slices. Heat 1 tablespoon olive oil in a large nonstick skillet over medium heat and cook the cheese for about 4 minutes, or until golden and crisp on both sides. Drain and pat dry with paper towels. Halve, peel, and seed ½ small watermelon and cut the flesh into small triangles. Toss the melon with a small bunch of chopped mint and the diced flesh of 1 ripe halved, seeded, and peeled avocado. Serve with the grilled haloumi. **Calories per serving 298**

fruity stuffed bell peppers

Calories per serving **421**
Preparation time **15 minutes**
Cooking time **1 hour**
Serves **4**

2 **red bell peppers**, cored, seeded, and halved
2 **orange bell peppers**, cored, seeded, and halved
2 tablespoons **olive oil**, plus extra for brushing
1 **red onion**, chopped
1 **garlic clove**, crushed
1 small **fresh red chile**, seeded and minced
3 tablespoons **pine nuts**
1¼ cups cooked **wild rice**
14-oz can **green lentils**, rinsed and drained
1½ cups **cherry tomatoes**, quartered
½ cup **ready-to-eat dried apricots**, chopped
handful of **golden raisins**
grated zest of 1 **lemon**
2 tablespoons chopped **mixed herbs**
3½ oz **feta cheese**, crumbled

Put the bell peppers in a baking dish, cut-side up, and brush each with a little oil. Place in a preheated oven at 400°F for 20 minutes.

Heat the oil in skillet, add the onion, garlic, and chile and fry for 2 minutes, then add the pine nuts and cook for a further 2 minutes, or until golden. Stir in all the remaining ingredients.

Remove the bell peppers from the oven and spoon the stuffing mixture into the bell peppers. Cover with foil, return to the oven, and cook for 25 minutes, then remove the foil and cook for a further 15 minutes. Serve with a crisp salad.

For fruity stuffed eggplant, roughly prick 2 large eggplants all over with a fork. Place on a cookie sheet and bake in a preheated oven at 400°F for 30 minutes. Remove from the oven and halve lengthwise, scoop out most of the flesh, and coarsely chop. Make the stuffing as above, adding the eggplant flesh to the pan with the onion, garlic, and chile. Spoon the mixture into the eggplant skins and cook as above. **Calories per serving 393**

okra & coconut stew

Calories per serving **421**
Serves **4**
Preparation time **15 minutes**
Cooking time **40 minutes**

12 oz **okra**
¼ cup **vegetable oil**, divided
2 **onions**, chopped
2 **green bell peppers**, cored, seeded, and cut into chunks
3 **celery stalks**, thinly sliced
3 **garlic cloves**, crushed
4 teaspoons **Cajun spice blend**
½ teaspoon **ground turmeric**
1¼ cups **vegetable stock**
14 fl oz can **coconut milk**
1¼ cups **frozen whole kernel corn**
juice of 1 **lime**
¼ cup chopped fresh **cilantro**
salt and **pepper**

Trim the stalk ends from the okra and cut the pods into ¾-inch pieces.

Heat 2 tablespoons of the oil in a large deep skillet and fry the okra for 5 minutes. Lift out with a slotted spoon and transfer to a plate.

Add the remaining oil to the skillet and very gently fry the onions, bell peppers, and celery, stirring frequently, for 10 minutes, or until softened but not browned. Add the garlic, spice blend, and turmeric and cook for 1 minute.

Pour in the stock and coconut milk and bring to a boil. Reduce the heat, cover, and cook gently for 10 minutes. Return the okra to the pan with the corn, lime juice, and cilantro and cook for a further 10 minutes. Season to taste with salt and pepper and serve.

For easy cornbread, to serve as an accompaniment, mix together 1 cup cornmeal, ¾ cup all-purpose flour, 1 teaspoon salt, 2 teaspoons baking powder, ½ teaspoon ground cumin, and ½ teaspoon dried red pepper flakes in a bowl. Beat 1 egg with 1 cup milk and add to the bowl. Mix gently until just combined (do not overmix). Add to a greased 6 x 4½ x 3-inch loaf pan. Bake in a preheated oven at 375°F for 30 minutes, or until firm to the touch. Serve warm or transfer to a wire rack to cool. **Calories per serving 272**

spinach & lima bean frittata

Calories per serving **432**
(not including salad)
Serves **2**
Preparation time **10 minutes**
Cooking time **10 minutes**

1 teaspoon **olive oil**
1 **onion**, sliced
14-oz can **lima beans**, rinsed and drained
7 oz **baby spinach**
4 **eggs**, beaten
2 oz **ricotta cheese**
salt (optional) and **black pepper**

Heat the oil in a medium skillet. Add the onion and fry for 3 to 4 minutes, or until softened. Add the lima beans and spinach and heat gently for 2 to 3 minutes, or until the spinach has wilted.

Pour in the eggs, then spoon over the ricotta and season with salt (if liked) and pepper. Cook until almost set, then place under a preheated hot broiler and cook for 1 to 2 minutes, or until golden and set. Serve with a tomato and red onion salad, if liked.

For Stilton & broccoli frittata, heat 1 teaspoon olive oil in a skillet and fry 1 sliced onion until softened. Add 1 cup small, lightly cooked broccoli florets and fry for 2 more minutes. Add the beaten eggs and scatter with 3 oz crumbled Stilton cheese. Cook as above until almost set, then transfer to a hot broiler and cook until golden. **Calories per serving 371**

eggplant parcels with pine nuts

Calories per serving **436**
Serves **2**
Preparation time **30 minutes, plus chilling**
Cooking time **12 to 15 minutes**

1 tablespoon **pine nuts**
1 long, large **eggplant**
4 oz **mozzarella cheese**
1 large or 2 small **plum tomatoes**
8 large **basil leaves**, plus extra, torn, to garnish
1 tablespoon **olive oil**
salt and **pepper**

Tomato dressing
2 tablespoons **olive oil**
1 teaspoon **balsamic vinegar**
1 teaspoon **sun-dried tomato paste**
1 teaspoon **lemon juice**

Make the dressing. Whisk together the oil, vinegar, tomato paste, and lemon juice in a small bowl. Set aside.

Dry-fry the pine nuts in a hot pan until golden brown. Remove from the pan and set aside.

Cut the stalk off of the eggplant and cut it lengthwise to give 8 slices (disregarding the ends). Put the slices in a pan of boiling salted water and cook for 2 minutes. Drain and dry on paper towels. Cut the mozzarella into 4 slices and the tomato into 8 slices (disregarding the outer edges).

Put 2 eggplant slices on dish in an X shape. Place a slice of tomato on top, season with salt and pepper, add a basil leaf, a slice of mozzarella, another basil leaf, then more salt and pepper, and finally another slice of tomato. Fold the edges of the eggplant around the filling to make a parcel. Repeat with the other ingredients until you have 4 parcels in total. Cover with plastic wrap and chill in the refrigerator for 20 minutes.

Place the eggplant parcels on a broiler rack and brush them with oil. Set the rack under a preheated hot broiler and cook the eggplant parcels for about 5 minutes on each side, or until golden brown. Serve 2 parcels per person, drizzled with the dressing, and scattered with the pine nuts and torn basil leaves.

For eggplant parcels with garlic bruschetta, drizzle 4 slices of ciabatta with 1 tablespoon olive oil and rub with garlic. Toast until golden. Make eggplant parcels as above and place one on each slice, top with Parmesan shavings, and scatter with 1 tablespoon toasted pine nuts. Omit the dressing. **Calories per serving 481**

sweet potato & coconut soup

Calories per serving **440**
Serves **4**
Preparation time **15 minutes**
Cooking time **30 minutes**

2 tablespoons **olive oil**
1 **onion**, minced
2 **garlic cloves**, crushed
1 teaspoon grated fresh **ginger root**
grated zest and juice of 1 **lime**
1 **red chile**, seeded and chopped
1½ lb **sweet potatoes**, peeled and coarsely chopped
2½ cups **vegetable stock**
14-oz can **coconut milk**
5 oz **baby spinach**
salt and **pepper**

Heat the oil in a saucepan, add the onion, garlic, ginger, lime zest, and chile and cook over low heat, stirring frequently, for 5 minutes, or until the onion is softened. Add the sweet potatoes and cook, stirring frequently, for 5 minutes.

Stir in the stock, coconut milk, lime juice, and salt and pepper. Bring to a boil, then reduce the heat, cover, and let simmer gently for 15 minutes, or until the potatoes are tender.

Transfer half the soup to a blender or food processor and blend until smooth. Return to the pan, stir in the spinach, and cook until just wilted. Adjust the seasoning and serve immediately.

For creamy pumpkin, cilantro & coconut soup, replace the sweet potato with an equal quantity of peeled, seeded, and diced pumpkin. Cook the soup for 20 minutes, then process in a blender or food processor until smooth, adding 2 tablespoons chopped fresh cilantro instead of the spinach. Continue the recipe as above. **Calories per serving 292**

crunchy thai-style salad

Calories per serving **440**
Serves **2**
Preparation time **10 minutes**

2 **carrots**
1 **zucchini**
½ small **red cabbage**, finely shredded
1 **yellow bell pepper**, cored, seeded, and thinly sliced
4 **scallions**, finely sliced
2 tablespoons chopped fresh **cilantro**
5 oz **rice noodles**

Dressing
1 **fresh red chile**, seeded and chopped
¼ cup **fish sauce**
grated zest and juice of **1 lime**
2 tablespoons **superfine sugar**

Use a potato peeler to shred the carrots and zucchini into fine slices. Toss together the sliced vegetables with the cabbage, pepper, scallions, and cilantro.

Cook the noodles in boiling water according to the instructions on the package, drain, and let cool.

Make the dressing by whisking together the chile, fish sauce, lime zest and juice, and sugar in a small bowl.

Mix the noodles with the vegetables. Toss the dressing through the salad and serve.

For crunchy coleslaw salad, toss together the sliced carrots, zucchini, cabbage, bell pepper, and scallions as above. In a separate bowl beat together 1 tablespoon crème fraîche, 1 tablespoon mayonnaise, 1 teaspoon mustard, and a good squeeze of lemon juice. Stir this dressing into the vegetables, scatter with ½ cup chopped fresh cilantro and serve. **Calories per serving 341**

arugula & goat cheese omelet

Calories per serving **461**
Serves **4**
Preparation time **5 minutes**
Cooking time **12 minutes**

12 **eggs**
¼ cup **milk**
¼ cup chopped **mixed herbs** (such as **chervil, chives, marjoram, parsley,** and **tarragon**)
3½ tablespoons **butter**, divided
4 oz diced **soft goat cheese**, divided
small handful of **baby arugula**, divided
salt and **pepper**

Beat the eggs, milk, herbs, and salt and pepper together in a large bowl. Melt one-quarter of the butter in an omelet pan. As soon as it stops foaming, swirl in one-quarter of the egg mixture and cook over medium heat, watching that it cooks evenly.

As soon as it is set on the underside but still a little runny in the center, scatter one-quarter of the cheese and one-quarter of the arugula over one half of the omelet. Carefully slide the omelet onto a warmed serving plate, folding it in half as you go. For the best results, serve immediately, then repeat to make 3 more omelets and serve each individually. Alternatively, keep warm in a moderate oven and serve all at the same time.

For cheese & tomato omelet, follow the recipe above to the end of the first stage. Then top each omelet with ½ oz shredded Cheddar cheese and ¼ cup halved cherry tomatoes. Carefully tip the omelet out onto a warmed plate, folding it in half as you go. Repeat to make 3 more omelets. **Calories per serving 427**

mixed bean salsa with tortilla chips

Calories per serving **469**
Serves **4**
Preparation time **10 minutes, plus standing**

2 x 13-oz cans **mixed beans**, rinsed and drained
3 **tomatoes**, chopped
1 **red bell pepper**, cored, seeded, and finely diced
6 **scallions**, sliced
1 teaspoon minced **fresh red chile**
2 tablespoons **olive oil**
1 tablespoon **white wine vinegar**
chopped **cilantro**, to garnish
salt and **pepper**

To serve
5 oz **tortilla chips**
½ cup **sour cream**

Put the beans, tomatoes, red bell pepper, and scallions into a food processor and blend until fairly smooth.

In a small bowl, whisk together the chile, oil, and vinegar, pour it over the bean mixture, and toss to coat. Season to taste with salt and pepper and garnish with cilantro. Cover and let stand at room temperature for about 30 minutes to allow the flavors to mingle.

Serve the salsa with tortilla chips and sour cream.

For mixed bean pilau, which will work as a substantial appetizer or side dish, add 1½ cups basmati rice to a pan, cover with 2½ cups water, and bring to a boil. Reduce the heat, cover, and simmer for 12 minutes without lifting off the lid. Remove from the heat, toss in the mixed bean salsa (see first stage above), and stir in 3 tablespoons chopped cilantro leaves. Replace the lid and return to very low heat for 5 minutes. Serve hot.
Calories per serving 483

roast vegetables & parsley pesto

Calories per serving **474**
Serves **4**
Preparation time **15 minutes**
Cooking time **50 minutes to 1 hour**

4 small **potatoes**, scrubbed
1 **red onion**
2 **carrots**
2 **parsnips**
8 **garlic cloves**, unpeeled
4 **thyme sprigs**
2 tablespoons **extra-virgin olive oil**

Parsley pesto
½ cup **blanched almonds**
large bunch of **flat-leaf parsley**
2 **garlic cloves**, chopped
½ cup **extra-virgin olive oil**
2 tablespoons grated **Parmesan cheese**
salt and **pepper**

Cut the potatoes and onion into wedges and the carrots and parsnips into quarters. Arrange in a single layer in a large, roomy roasting pan. Add the garlic cloves, thyme sprigs, oil, and salt and pepper and stir well to coat evenly. Roast in a preheated oven at 425°F for 50 minutes to 1 hour, or until browned and tender. Stir halfway through.

Make the pesto. Heat a heavy skillet until hot, add the almonds, and dry-fry over medium heat, stirring, for 3 to 4 minutes, or until browned. Transfer to a bowl and let cool.

Put the almonds in a mortar or food processor, add the parsley, garlic, and salt and pepper and grind with a pestle or process to form a coarse paste. Transfer to a bowl, stir in the oil and Parmesan, and adjust the seasoning.

Serve the roast vegetables hot with the pesto.

mango curry

Calories per serving **474**
Serves **4**
Preparation time **10 minutes**
Cooking time **8 to 10 minutes**

1 tablespoon **vegetable oil**
1 teaspoon **mustard seeds**
1 **onion**, halved and thinly sliced
15 to 20 **curry leaves**, fresh or dried
½ teaspoon **dried red pepper flakes**
1 teaspoon peeled and grated fresh **ginger root**
1 **green chile**, seeded and sliced
1 teaspoon **ground turmeric**
3 ripe **mangoes**, peeled, seeded, and thinly sliced
1¾ cups **plain yogurt**, lightly beaten
salt
4 **chapatis**, to serve

Heat the oil in a large saucepan until hot, add the mustard seeds, onion, curry leaves, and dried red pepper flakes and fry, stirring, for 4 to 5 minutes, or until the onion is lightly browned.

Add the ginger and green chile and stir-fry for 1 minute, then add the turmeric and stir to combine.

Remove the pan from the heat, add the mangoes and yogurt, and stir continuously until well mixed. Season to taste with salt. Return the pan to low heat and heat through for 1 minute, stirring continuously. (Do not let it boil or the curry will curdle.) Serve immediately with 4 warm chapatis.

For eggplant & pea curry, heat 3 tablespoons sunflower oil in a large skillet until hot, then add 4 peeled and cubed medium-sized potatoes, 1 eggplant, cut into small chunks, 1 cup frozen peas, 2 finely sliced onions, 2 crushed garlic cloves, 1 tablespoon ginger paste, and 2 tablespoons medium curry powder. Stir-fry for 3 to 4 minutes, or until the onion has softened and is turning golden, then add 2½ cups vegetable stock and cook for 10 to 15 minutes, or until the stock has reduced. Stir in ½ cup crème fraîche and serve with a mini naan bread. **Calories per serving 482**

tomato, avocado & peach salad

Calories per serving **477**
Serves **4**
Preparation time **15 minutes**, plus cooling
Cooking time **20 minutes**

4 **plum tomatoes**, sliced
1 **avocado**, peeled, seeded, and sliced
7 oz **buffalo mozzarella cheese**, sliced
1 ripe **peach**, stoned and diced
½ cup pitted **black olives**
1 **fresh red chile**, seeded and minced
3 tablespoons **extra-virgin olive oil**
juice of 1 **lime**
1 tablespoon chopped fresh **cilantro**
salt and **pepper**

Balsamic glaze
2½ cups **balsamic vinegar**

First make the balsamic glaze. Pour the vinegar into a saucepan and bring to a boil. Reduce the heat and let simmer gently for 20 minutes, or until reduced to about ½ cup. Let cool completely.

Arrange the tomatoes, avocado, and mozzarella on a large platter. Combine the peach, olives, chile, oil, lime juice, cilantro, and salt and pepper in a bowl, stir well, and spoon evenly over the salad.

Drizzle the salad with the balsamic glaze and serve.

For classic Italian tricolore salad, arrange 4 sliced plum tomatoes, 1 sliced avocado, 7 oz sliced buffalo mozzarella, and a few torn basil leaves on a platter. Drizzle with some extra-virgin olive oil and a little white wine vinegar, and season with salt and cracked black pepper. **Calories per serving 324**

roasted bell peppers with quinoa

Calories per serving **489**
Serves **4**
Preparation time **15 minutes**
Cooking time **45 minutes**

2 **romano** or **long red bell peppers**, halved, cored, and seeded
2 large **yellow bell peppers**, halved, cored, and seeded
20 **red** and **yellow cherry tomatoes**, halved
1 teaspoon **cumin seeds**
2 tablespoons **olive oil**, divided
1 cup **quinoa**
1 **onion**, minced
½ teaspoon **ground ginger**
1 teaspoon **paprika**
pinch of **nutmeg**
¼ cup **ready-to-eat dried apricots**, chopped
¼ cup **pitted dates**, chopped
⅓ cup shelled **pistachio nuts**
¼ cup **flaked almonds**, toasted, plus extra to garnish
2 **scallions**, finely sliced
salt and **pepper**

Fill the red bell pepper halves with the yellow cherry tomatoes and the yellow bell pepper halves with the red cherry tomatoes. Scatter with the cumin seeds, drizzle with 1 tablespoon of the oil, and season well with salt and pepper. Place in a preheated oven at 350°F for about 45 minutes, or until tender and slightly blackened around the edges.

Rinse the quinoa several times in cold water. Pour into a pan with twice its volume of boiling water, cover, and simmer for about 12 minutes. (It is cooked when the seed is coming away from the germ.) Remove from the heat, cover, and let stand until all the water has been absorbed.

Heat the remaining oil in a small skillet over medium heat, add the onion, and cook for 10 minutes, or until softened. Add the spices and dried fruits and nuts and cook for a further 3 to 4 minutes, or until the fruits have softened, stirring frequently. Gently fold the mixture into the cooked quinoa.

Heap the quinoa onto 4 plates and top each with 1 red and 1 yellow pepper half. Scatter with the scallions and extra flaked almonds and serve.

For quinoa-stuffed bell peppers, make the fruit and nut quinoa as above. Cut 10 cherry tomatoes into quarters and mix with the quinoa. Spoon into the halved bell peppers and top with 3 oz sliced reduced-fat feta or goat cheese. Drizzle with a little olive oil and season with salt and pepper. Place in the oven for 45 minutes, or until the bell peppers are tender. Serve as above with salad leaves. **Calories per serving 495**

haloumi with pomegranate salsa

Calories per serving **490**
Serves **4**
Preparation time **10 minutes**
Cooking time **5 minutes**

14½ oz **haloumi cheese**, sliced
1 tablespoon **honey**

Pomegranate salsa
½ **pomegranate**
¼ cup **extra-virgin olive oil**
2 tablespoons chopped **parsley**
1 tablespoon **lemon juice**
1 small **fresh red chile**, seeded and minced
1 small **garlic clove**, crushed
1 teaspoon **pomegranate syrup** (optional)
salt and **pepper**

First make the pomegranate salsa. Carefully scoop the pomegranate seeds into a bowl, discarding all the white membrane. Stir in the remaining ingredients and season with salt and pepper.

Heat a large nonstick skillet for 2 to 3 minutes, or until hot. Add the haloumi slices, in batches, and cook over high heat for about 60 seconds on each side, or until browned and softened.

Warm the honey in a small saucepan until runny.

Transfer the pan-fried haloumi to serving plates and spoon over the salsa. Drizzle the haloumi and salsa with the honey and serve immediately.

For avocado salsa, peel, seed, and finely dice 1 small ripe avocado and combine with 4 minced scallions, 1 tablespoon lemon juice, 1 tablespoon chopped fresh cilantro, and salt and pepper to taste. **Calories per serving 435**

spinach & gorgonzola salad

Calories per serving **495**
Serves **4**
Preparation time **5 minutes, plus cooling**
Cooking time **3 minutes**

1 tablespoon **honey**
1¼ cups **walnut halves**
8 oz **green snap beans**, trimmed
7 oz **baby spinach**
5 oz **Gorgonzola cheese**, crumbled

Dressing
3 tablespoons **walnut oil**
1 tablespoon **extra-virgin olive oil**
1 to 2 tablespoons **sherry vinegar**
salt and **pepper**

Heat the honey in a small skillet, add the walnuts, and stir-fry over medium heat for 2 to 3 minutes, or until the nuts are glazed. Transfer to a plate and let cool.

Meanwhile, cook the green beans in a saucepan of lightly salted boiling water for 3 minutes. Drain, refresh under cold water, and shake dry. Put in a large bowl with the spinach leaves.

Whisk all the dressing ingredients together in a small bowl and season with salt and pepper. Pour evenly over the salad and toss well. Arrange the salad in serving bowls, scatter with the Gorgonzola and glazed walnuts, and serve immediately.

For watercress, almond & Stilton salad, replace the spinach with an equal weight of watercress. Dress with ½ cup toasted sliced almonds instead of the honeyed walnuts, 7 oz crumbled Stilton instead of the Gorgonzola, and a drizzle of olive oil. **Calories per serving 318**

creamy zucchini with walnuts

Calories per serving **495**
Serves **4**
Preparation time **10 minutes**
Cooking time **10 to 15 minutes**

3 tablespoons **olive oil**
1 **onion**, chopped
4 **zucchini**, cut into matchsticks
2 **celery stalks**, cut into matchsticks
8 oz **soft cheese with garlic**
¾ cup **walnut pieces**
salt and **pepper**

Heat the oil in a large skillet, add the onion, and cook for 5 minutes, or until soft. Add the zucchini and celery and cook for 4 to 5 minutes, or until soft and beginning to brown.

Add the cheese and cook for 2 to 3 minutes, or until melted. Stir in the walnuts, season to taste with salt and pepper, and serve immediately.

For curried zucchini, cook the onion as above, then add 2 small, quartered potatoes and cook for 2 to 3 minutes. Stir in the zucchini, sliced, with ½ teaspoon chili powder, ½ teaspoon turmeric, 1 teaspoon ground coriander, and ½ teaspoon salt. Add ½ cup water, cover, and cook over low heat for 8 to 10 minutes, or until the potatoes are tender.
Calories per serving 198

index

almonds 232
fennel & almond soup 114
apples
arugula, apple & balsamic salad 22
spicy apple & parsnip soup 108
spicy apple & potato soup 108
spicy apple relish 80
apricots
smoked tofu & apricot sausages 80
artichokes
Italian bean & artichoke salad 182
roasted artichoke & pepper hummus 192
arugula
arugula & goat cheese omelet 218
arugula & Parmesan salad 60
arugula, apple & balsamic salad 22
arugula, pear & pecorino salad 22
arugula salad with chive dressing 60
asparagus 186
charred asparagus salad with pine nuts 166

balsamic dressing 22, 52
basil 118
beans
baked tortillas with fava bean hummus 144
braised black cabbage & borlotti 24
broccoli & black-eyed pea curry 30
cannellini with sage & tomato 34
cheesy squash, bell pepper & mixed bean soup 28
fig, bean & toasted pecan salad 176
home-baked beans 128
home-baked beans with baked potatoes 128
Italian bean & artichoke salad 182
lima bean & tomato soup 184
mixed bean pilau 220
mixed bean salad 176
mixed bean salsa with tortilla chips 220
quick bean & feta salad 182
Spanish white bean soup 42
spinach & lima bean frittata 210
squash, kale & mixed bean soup 28
white bean & sun-dried tomato salad 102
white bean soup Provençal 42
beer 136
beets
beet & chickpea salad 188
beet dressing 58
beet, spinach & goat cheese salad 82
beet, spinach & orange salad 82
spiced beet salad 44
trivandrum beet curry 44
Belgian endive
Belgian endive & baby romaine salad 130
grilled radicchio & Belgian endive salad 168
bell peppers
bell pepper & eggplant hummus 192
caper & lemon peperonata 54
cheesy roasted bell peppers 152
cheesy squash, bell pepper & mixed bean soup 28
chickpea & bell pepper salad 178
corn & bell pepper frittata 172
fruity stuffed bell peppers 206
peperonata 54
quinoa-stuffed bell peppers 228
roasted artichoke & bell pepper hummus 192
roasted bell peppers with quinoa 228
roasted stuffed bell peppers 152
split pea & bell pepper patties 196
zucchini, bell pepper & Gruyère frittata 172
body mass index (BMI) 10
bok choy
bok choy with chile & ginger 64
bok choy with water chestnuts & garlic 104
veggie stir-fry with bok choy 26
broccoli
broccoli & black-eyed pea curry 30
Italian broccoli & egg salad 110
Stilton & broccoli frittata 210

cabbage
braised black cabbage & borlotti 24
chile cabbage 50
crunchy coleslaw salad 216
crunchy slaw with sweet chili sauce 40
curried cabbage & carrot stir-fry 68
red cabbage slaw 40
speedy coconut, carrot & cabbage curry 68
calories 8, 10–11
how many calories do we need? 11
losing weight 12–13
caper & lemon peperonata 54
carbohydrates 17
carrots
carrot & cashew salad 132
carrot & celery root coleslaw 132
speedy coconut, carrot & cabbage curry 68
spiced carrot & lentil soup 184
spicy squash & carrot soup 116
squash, carrot & mango tagine 116
cashews 132
cauliflower
cauliflower & chickpea curry 30
curried cauliflower with chickpeas 158
Malaysian spicy cauliflower 46
spicy cauliflower soup 46
celery root
carrot & celery root coleslaw 132
Cheddar 16
cheese 15–16
arugula & goat cheese omelet 218
arugula & Parmesan salad 60
arugula, pear & pecorino salad 22
baked figs with goat cheese 72

beet, spinach & goat cheese salad 82
cheese & tomato omelet 218
cheesy roasted bell peppers 152
cheesy squash, bell pepper & mixed bean soup 28
eggplant, tomato & feta rolls 112
figs stuffed with mozzarella & basil 72
Gorgonzola, pecan & pear salad 130
Greek country salad with haloumi 190
grilled zucchini with lemon, mint & Parmesan 126
grilled vegetable & haloumi salad 204
haloumi with pomegranate salsa 230
lentil & feta salad 186
quick bean & feta salad 182
sage & goat cheese frittata 86
spinach & goat cheese frittata 86
spinach & Gorgonzola salad 232
Stilton & broccoli frittata 210
tomato & mozzarella salad 78
walnut & blue cheese salad 168
watercress, almond & Stilton salad 232
watermelon & haloumi salad 204
watermelon, fennel & feta salad 106
zucchini & mozzarella rolls 112
zucchini, bell pepper & Gruyère frittata 172
zucchini, feta & mint salad 36
zucchini, pea & cheese frittata 74
chermoula tofu & roasted vegetables 92
chestnuts
parsnip, sage & chestnut soup 148
chickpeas
baked tortillas with hummus 144
beet & chickpea salad 188
cauliflower & chickpea curry 30
chickpea & bell pepper salad 178
chickpea & chile salad 102
chickpea & herb salad 188
curried cauliflower with chickpeas 158
spicy lentils & chickpeas 122
chiles
bok choy with chile & ginger 64
chickpea & chile salad 102
chile cabbage 50
chile dressing 32
chile kale 50
crunchy slaw with chili sauce 40
homemade chile oil 148
pickled cucumber & chile salad 76
stir-fried tofu with basil & chile 118
sweet chili vegetable stir-fry 26
vegetables with sweet chili sauce 38
chive dressing 60
choy sum, garlicky 104
cilantro 214
cilantro dressing 198

coconut
creamy pumpkin, cilantro & coconut soup 214
Malaysian coconut vegetables 98
speedy coconut, carrot & cabbage curry 68
sweet potato & coconut soup 214
corn & pepper frittata 172
cornbread, easy 208
croutons 124, 190
cucumber
cucumber & dill salad 52
garden salad 48
pickled cucumber & chile salad 76
strawberry & cucumber salad 52
tzatziki 164, 178, 196

dairy alternatives 17
dairy products 17
diet, balanced 16–17
improving 13–14
vegetarian 14–15
dill
cucumber & dill salad 52

eggplant
baked eggplant with tzatziki 164
bell pepper & eggplant hummus 192
eggplant & pea curry 224
eggplant parcels with garlic bruschetta 212
eggplant parcels with pine nuts 212
eggplant, tomato & feta rolls 112
fruity stuffed eggplant 206
spicy eggplant curry 90
eggs
cheese & tomato omelet 218

corn & bell pepper frittata 172
Italian broccoli & egg salad 110
lentil salad with poached egg & asparagus 186
poached eggs & spinach 134
rocket & goat cheese omelet 218
sage & goat cheese frittata 86
spinach & lima bean frittata 210
spinach & pea frittata 74
Stilton & broccoli frittata 210
zucchini, pea & cheese frittata 74
zucchini, pepper & Gruyère frittata 172
exercise 11–12

fats 13
fennel
fennel & almond soup with orange & olive gremolata 114
fennel & orange casserole 88
fennel gratin 88
fennel soup with olive gremolata 114
fennel, orange & parsley salad 106
pickled fennel salad 66
shaved fennel & radish salad 66
watermelon, fennel & feta salad 106
feta 15–16, 36, 106, 112, 182, 186
figs
baked figs with goat cheese 72
fig, bean & toasted pecan salad 176
figs stuffed with mozzarella & basil 72

fruit 17
  fruity stuffed bell peppers 206
  fruity stuffed eggplant 206
  fruity summer smoothie 20
  sweet quinoa porridge with banana & dates 140

garden cress
  spinach, egg & garden cress salad 134
garlic
  bok choy with water chestnuts & garlic 104
  garlic & caramelized onion bhajis 194
  garlic bruschetta 212
  garlic croutons 124
  garlicky choy sum 104
ginger 64
gnocchi with walnut pesto as an appetizer 160
goat cheese 15, 72, 82, 86, 218

hazelnuts 166
herbs
  chickpea & herb salad 188
  herb & yogurt chutney 194

ingredients 15

kale
  chile kale 50
  squash, kale & mixed bean soup 28

leeks
  cream of leek & pea soup 162
  cream of leek, pea & watercress soup 162
  creamed leek salad with hazelnuts 166

lemon
  caper & lemon peperonata 54
  grilled zucchini with lemon, mint & Parmesan 126
lentils
  lentil & feta salad 186
  lentil moussaka 170
  lentil salad with poached egg & asparagus 186
  spiced carrot & lentil soup 184
  spicy lentils & chickpeas 122
lettuce
  Belgian endive & baby romaine salad 130
  garden salad 48
  Thai salad wraps 32

mango
  homemade mango chutney 158
  mango curry 224
  soy milk & mango shake 20
  squash, carrot & mango tagine 116
milk 8, 13
  fruity summer smoothie 20
minerals 17
mint
  grilled zucchini with lemon, mint & Parmesan 126
  zucchini, feta & mint salad 36
moussaka & baked potatoes 170
mozzarella 16, 72, 78, 112
mushrooms
  green curry with straw mushrooms 84
  marinated tofu & mushroom salad 56
  mushroom pasta salad 174

mushroom soup with garlic croutons 124
mushroom stroganoff 124
mushrooms à la grecque 174
stuffed mushrooms with tofu 94
tofu & mushroom pasta 94

noodles
  one-pot tofu & vegetable noodles 180

oats
  porridge with prune compote 140
obesity 10
okra & coconut stew 208
okra, pea & tomato curry 62
olives
  fennel & almond soup with orange & olive gremolata 114
  fennel soup with olive gremolata 114
  gremolata 114
  pumpkin soup with olive salsa 120
onions
  garlic & caramelized onion bhajis 194
orange
  beet, spinach & orange salad 82
  fennel & almond soup with orange & olive gremolata 114
  fennel & orange casserole 88
  fennel, orange & parsley salad 106
oyster sauce 118

Parmesan
  Parmesan 16, 60, 126

Parmesan toast 100
parsley 106
  parsley pesto 222
parsnips
  parsnip, sage & chestnut soup 148
  spicy apple & parsnip soup 108
pasta
  mushroom pasta salad 174
  roasted vegetable pasta sauce 146
  tofu & mushroom pasta 94
  tomato & pasta salad 78
peaches
  tomato, avocado & peach salad 226
pears
  arugula, pear & pecorino salad 22
  Gorgonzola, pecan & pear salad 130
peas
  cream of leek & pea soup 162
  cream of leek, pea & watercress soup 162
  eggplant & pea curry 224
  okra, pea & tomato curry 62
  spiced seeded pea & tomato pilaf 62
  spinach & pea frittata 74
  split pea & bell pepper patties 196
  Thai squash, tofu & pea curry 154
  zucchini, pea & cheese frittata 74
pecans
  fig, bean & toasted pecan salad 176
  Gorgonzola, pecan & pear salad 130
pine nuts 24, 166, 212
pomegranate salsa 230

potatoes
  home-baked beans with baked potatoes 128
  moussaka on baked potatoes 170
  spicy apple & potato soup 108
protein 16–17
prunes
  porridge with prune compote 140
pumpkin
  creamy pumpkin, cilantro & coconut soup 214
  Indian spiced pumpkin wedges 138
  pumpkin soup with olive salsa 120
  pumpkin with walnut pesto 160

quinoa
  quinoa-stuffed bell peppers 228
  roasted bell peppers with quinoa 228
  sweet quinoa porridge with banana & dates 140

radicchio
  grilled radicchio & Belgian endive salad 168
radishes
  shaved fennel & radish salad 66
ratatouille, quick one-pot 150
rice
  mixed bean pilau 220
  spiced seeded pea & tomato pilaf 62
  tofu & rice salad 56
  vegetable & rice soup 136
ricotta 16

sage
  cannellini with sage & tomato 34
  parsnip, sage & chestnut soup 148
  sage & goat cheese frittata 86
soy milk & mango shake 20
spinach
  beet, spinach & goat cheese salad 82
  beet, spinach & orange salad 82
  poached eggs & spinach 134
  spinach & goat cheese frittata 86
  spinach & Gorgonzola salad 232
  spinach & lima bean frittata 210
  spinach & pea frittata 74
  spinach, egg & garden cress salad 134
  spinach with pine nuts 24
squash
  cheesy squash, bell pepper & mixed bean soup 28
  roasted butternut squash soup 120
  spicy squash & carrot soup 116
  squash, carrot & mango tagine 116
  squash, kale & mixed bean soup 28
  Thai squash, tofu & pea curry 154
strawberry & cucumber salad 52
sweet potatoes
  baked sweet potatoes 202
  crispy sweet potato skins 202
  Indian-spiced sweet potato wedges 138
  sweet potato & coconut soup 214
  sweet potatoes & tomato salsa 198
  sweet potatoes with cilantro dressing 198

taleggio 16
tofu
  chermoula tofu & roasted vegetables 92
  marinated tofu & mushroom salad 56
  one-pot tofu & vegetable noodles 180
  smoked tofu & apricot sausages 80
  stir-fried tofu with basil & chile 118
  stuffed mushrooms with tofu 94
  Thai red tofu & vegetable curry 180
  Thai squash, tofu & pea curry 154
  tofu & mushroom pasta 94
  tofu & rice salad 56
  tofu & vegetables in oyster sauce 118
tomatoes
  cannellini with sage & tomato 34
  cheese & tomato omelet 218
  eggplant, tomato & feta rolls 112
  garden salad 48
  lima bean & tomato soup 184
  okra, pea & tomato curry 62
  spiced seeded pea & tomato pilaf 62
  spiced tomato sauce 164
  sweet potatoes & tomato salsa 198
  tomato & mozzarella salad 78
  tomato & pasta salad 78
  tomato, avocado & peach salad 226
  white bean & sun-dried tomato salad 102
tortillas
  baked tortillas with fava bean hummus 144
  baked tortillas with hummus 144
  tortilla chips 220

vegetables 17
  chermoula tofu & roasted vegetables 92
  classic Italian tricolore salad 226
  country Thai-style salad 216
  Greek country salad with chunky croutons 190
  Greek country salad with haloumi 190
  Greek vegetable casserole 156
  grilled vegetable & haloumi salad 204
  grilled vegetable platter 126
  homemade vegetable stock 96
  Malaysian coconut vegetables 98
  Middle Eastern vegetable casserole 156
  one-pot tofu & vegetable noodles 180
  pickled vegetable salad 76
  quick one-pot ratatouille 150
  roast vegetables & parsley pesto 222
  roasted summer vegetables 146

roasted vegetable pasta sauce 146
spring minestrone 100
spring vegetable salad 58
summer vegetable soup 96
sweet chili vegetable stir-fry 26
Thai green vegetable curry 154
Thai red tofu & vegetable curry 180
Thai vegetable salad 32
tofu & vegetables in oyster sauce 118
vegetable & rice soup 136
vegetable korma 84
vegetables with sweet chili sauce 38
veggie stir-fry with bok choy 26
winter vegetable & beer broth 136
vegetarian pasta cheese 16
Vegetarian Society 14
vitamins 17

walnuts 234
walnut & blue cheese salad 168
walnut pesto 160
water chestnuts 104
watercress
 cream of leek, pea & watercress soup 162
watercress, almond & Stilton salad 232
watermelon & haloumi salad 204
watermelon, fennel & feta salad 106
weight 10, 12–13

yogurt 8, 13
cooling, spiced yogurt 122
herb & yogurt chutney 194
yogurt dressing 40

zucchini
creamy zucchini with walnuts 234
curried zucchini 234
grilled zucchini with lemon, mint & Parmesan 126
marinated zucchini salad 36
zucchini & mozzarella rolls 112
zucchini, bell pepper & Gruyère frittata 172
zucchini, feta & mint salad 36
zucchini, pea & cheese frittata 74

acknowledgments

Executive editor: Eleanor Maxfield
Senior editor: Leanne Bryan
Designer: Eoghan O'Brien
Nutritionist: Angela Dowden
Assistant production manager: Caroline Alberti

Octopus Publishing Group Frank Adam 95, 213; Stephen Conroy 2, 9, 12, 18, 25, 35, 43, 55, 70, 75, 83, 85, 99, 109, 125, 127, 145, 151, 157, 159, 171, 173, 175, 183, 205, 217, 221, 225, 235; Will Heap 10, 31, 39, 45, 47, 63, 65, 69, 105; Jeremy Hopley 41; William Lingwood 87, 111, 153, 161; Neil Mersh 53, 103, 113; Emma Neish 195; Lis Parsons 4, 6, 11, 15, 21, 23, 37, 49, 57, 59, 61, 67, 77, 79, 81, 91, 93, 101, 131, 142, 165, 169, 179, 187, 189, 197, 200; William Reavell 51, 181, 185; Craig Robertson 199; Gareth Sambidge 97, 211; William Shaw 1, 8, 13, 17, 27, 29, 117, 123, 133, 135, 141, 147, 149, 163, 177, 193, 207, 209, 229, 231; Ian Wallace 14, 33, 73, 89, 107, 115, 119, 121, 129, 137, 139, 155, 167, 191, 203, 215, 219, 223, 227, 233.